J.D.B.
...itics of the third

CHATHAM HOUSE ESSAYS: 15

THE POLITICS OF THE THIRD WORLD

CHATHAM HOUSE ESSAYS

Previous essays in the series have been:

1 *The Chinese View of Their Place in the World.* By C. P. FitzGerald

2 *The China-India Border: The Origins of the Disputed Boundaries.* By Alastair Lamb

3 *The Debatable Alliance: An Essay in Anglo-American Relations.* By Coral Bell

4 *Sterling in the Sixties.* By Christopher McMahon

5 *Ballot Box and Bayonet: People and Government in Emergent Asian Countries.* By Hugh Tinker

6 *Imperial Outpost—Aden: Its Place in British Strategic Policy.* By Gillian King

7 *Changing Perspectives in British Foreign Policy.* By Kenneth Younger

8 *What Kind of Europe? The Community since De Gaulle's Veto.* By Miriam Camps

9 *Republic under Pressure: A Study of South African Foreign Policy.* By J. E. Spence

10 *The Arab Cold War 1958–1964: A Study of Ideology in Politics.* By Malcolm Kerr

11 *Vatican Politics. At the Second Vatican Council 1962–5.* By George Bull

12 *Trade Policies for Britain: A Study in Alternatives.* By S. J. Wells

13 *The Uneasy Entente. French Foreign Policy and Franco-British Misunderstandings.* By Dorothy Pickles

14 *Towards Peace in Indo-China.* By Anthony Eden, Earl of Avon.

The Institute gratefully acknowledges the comments and suggestions of the following who read the manuscript on behalf of the Research Committee: Dennis Austin, Professor Geoffrey Goodwin, Professor W. H. Morris Jones, and Susan Strange.

The Politics of the Third World

BY

J. D. B. MILLER

Issued under the auspices of the Royal Institute of International Affairs

OXFORD UNIVERSITY PRESS

LONDON NEW YORK TORONTO

1966

Oxford University Press, Ely House, London W.1

GLASGOW NEW YORK TORONTO MELBOURNE WELLINGTON
CAPE TOWN SALISBURY IBADAN NAIROBI LUSAKA ADDIS ABABA
BOMBAY CALCUTTA MADRAS KARACHI LAHORE DACCA
KUALA LUMPUR HONG KONG TOKYO

Printed in Great Britain by
The Bowering Press, Plymouth

For

TOBY

A world in himself

Contents

Abbreviations*

AAPO: All-African People's Organization
AAPSO: Afro-Asian People's Solidarity Organization
ASA: Association of Southeast Asia
OAU: Organization of African Unity
UAM: Union Africaine et Malgache
UNCTAD: United Nations Conference on Trade and Development

* i.e. less commonly used abbreviations

Introduction

'THE Third World' is a cant phrase, derived from the French *tiers monde* and used to describe those countries which are plainly neither Communist nor Western. Some countries clearly belong to it and others, just as clearly, do not: India and Indonesia are undoubtedly in, Norway and Australia undoubtedly out. Problems of definition arise, however, not with these obvious cases, but with the marginal ones, of which we may choose Israel and Japan as examples. Neither is usually spoken of as belonging to the Third World. In Israel's case this is largely because of the policy of deliberate estrangement which the Arab states have pursued: they have objected to Israel's inclusion in any association of Afro-Asian countries, and states which wished to obtain their goodwill have usually acquiesced. Another reason, however, is that Israel, while now having a population which is heavily 'oriental' in origin, was founded by European Jews and has retained a strongly European character. In the case of Japan the reasons for doubt about inclusion in the Third World are quite different. Japan is undoubtedly Asian and provided, in its defeat of Russia in 1905, a stimulus to Asian nationalist movements such as they had not had before; but its 'imperialist' activities in China and Southeast Asia alienated many nationalists in the 1930s and 1940s, and its present position as one of the 'developed' countries, with a substantial modern economy, sets it apart from countries which are still striving to break out of the limits imposed by traditional agriculture. It does, however, attend Afro-Asian meetings.

Certain changes would be needed for these two countries to be fully accepted as Third World members. If it were possible to make peace between Israel and the Arab states, an approach from Israel to participate in Afro-Asian activities would presumably be accepted. If the present Japanese government were replaced by a Social-Democratic one which repudiated the American alliance and declared itself non-aligned, there would be many more states to wish it welcome in spite of its wealth; Kuwait, with the highest income per head in the world, is not denied entry on Afro-Asian occasions. But there would still be a feeling that these two countries did not conform to the rough pattern of identity of Third World countries, which is formed by three main characteristics: being non-European, being non-Communist, and being poor.

By and large, the Third World is defined here as comprising those countries of Asia and Africa which are not under the control of Europeans and do not have Communist governments. The great majority are former colonies. The major omission is Latin America. My main reason for leaving it out is ignorance: I do not know enough about it. In addition, however, it seems to me reasonable to regard Latin America as something of a Fourth World, with characteristics of its own which entitle it to be studied in its own right and not forced to conform to whatever generalizations can be made about the Third. Latin American independence preceded by more than a century the movement which has led to the vast post-war increase in independent states in Asia and Africa. The intervening period gave Latin America a form of experience which marked it off from other parts of the world. Its predominant culture was Latin, not indigenous; its dominant groups were European in origin; its relations with the United States, ever since the enunciation of the Monroe Doctrine, have been unique in world affairs, and remain unparalleled in the experience of Asia and Africa; its own interrelationships have been its main field of international concern, forming a distinct area of world politics, largely untouched by outside forces except that of the United States; and, even now, direct involvement of Latin America with the Afro-Asian countries is minimal, although it may be greater in future.

The last of these points about Latin America is of special importance when we are trying to identify the Third World as a political entity. As I have said, the countries of the Third World are non-European, non-Communist, and poor, but these characteristics would not have been enough in themselves for identification, if there had not also been some degree of political agreement amongst the countries concerned. More than anything else, the common fronts which Afro-Asian countries have presented, or seemed to present, at the United Nations and at Bandung, in the OAU and the Arab League, have created the impression of a distinctive political force—or, more accurately, of a number of political forces to which unity is a prime aspiration. The main point made in this book is that such unity has neither been shown in practice nor is likely to reveal itself in the future. Afro-Asian unity is something which orators such as President Sukarno invoke to solve their own problems. Arab unity and African unity are the same. Each of these is a pious wish; none can be relied upon in action.

Yet it is the constant attempt to make realities of them that enables us to use the cant phrase Third World as something more than a journalist's tag. There are profound differences of condition and aim between the Third World countries and those of other worlds, especially the Western and Communist. The fact of their being poor is a potential source of unity: it alienates them from rich countries, whether these have capitalist or socialist bases for their economies; it also prompts them to seek common goals if these seem likely to benefit all of them. It is also, of course, a source of disunity. While all are poor, some are much poorer than others, which do not wish to fall to their level; moreover, competition between them for aid and investment from the richer countries is a potent source of friction. But the general effect of poverty is to set them apart from those developed economies which most Western countries have achieved and towards which Communist countries are driving. The same is true of their generally anti-colonialist character, arising from the fact that so many of them were until recently colonies of Western powers. This anti-colonialism unites through its emotional force, but has its divisive quality in the different perspectives which the various new states derive from their colonial experience. Yet the sense of outrage which anti-colonialism involves cannot be shared in the same emotional way by Western countries, and is alien to most Communist countries, in spite of the dogmatic views with which they support it; only the Asian minority (China, North Korea, and North Vietnam) can share it.

The point is that there is enough in the assumptions and emotions of Afro-Asian states to warrant our treating them as a unit for purposes of study, so long as we do not mistake slogans for facts or aspirations for achievements. Many Third World leaders *want* the Third World to be a unit for certain purposes; the question is whether it ever is, and, if it is not, why not. The answer of this essay is that it hardly ever is, but that the process of trying to make it one has had important effects on the style and content of the diplomacy of Third World countries. The dominant element in their diplomacy in each case is, however, the burgeoning sense of their individual national interest which comes with their experience of international politics. They have Afro-Asian spheres within which their main concern is their relations with one another; but the total effect of their experience is to urge them towards more specific and circumspect definitions of what is best for their individual selves. That is, they become more and more like other states in their behaviour.

This is an essay, not a treatise, and I have tried to keep scholarly apparatus to a minimum. I am grateful to Chatham House for giving me the opportunity to write it, and generous facilities in the process; study leave from my university in Canberra gave me the time in which to undertake it. I should like to acknowledge the help I have had from conversations with my colleague, Dr T. B. Millar, with whom I journeyed to Algiers in June 1965, in an abortive attempt to attend the 'second Bandung'. Certain research was done for us before we left by Mrs Elizabeth MacFarlane and Mrs Joan Davidson; I have found this helpful in the present undertaking. My wife has, as usual, been the most important element in enabling me to do this work.

I

Mostly New States

THE countries of the Third World are often given a flat uniformity by statements that they are all caught up in a revolution, or that they are all poor, or that they all take the same line towards the Western and Communist worlds. These mistaken views obscure the very great variety of states in Africa and Asia. They are mostly new, in the sense that they have been established since World War II, but they also include states of considerable experience, such as Afghanistan, Iran, Thailand, Egypt, and Ethiopia. The new states attract the most attention, because of their very newness; but the older ones, and those, such as India and Burma, which have now had nearly two decades of independence, matter a great deal in setting the tone of joint Afro-Asian effort and discussion.

Since this book is concerned with international behaviour, not with the process of development within individual states, most attention will be devoted to those aspects of a state's domestic affairs that contribute towards its foreign policy. For new states, the most important domestic resources brought to bear on international matters are often those derived from previous colonial control. In every case, colonialism involved some degree of forced modernization. It was never complete, and in many instances it brought about glaring contrasts between old and new practices; but it generally had most influence in those fields in which the new state, once established, wished to develop.

Colonial influence

Indeed, experience under colonialism often provides the only effective base on which development can proceed, even in those states which are least tolerant of the colonial idea. In military matters, for example, no new state will wish to return to the elephant as a means of transport or the assegai as a missile. Nor will it consider that traditional forms of military leadership are suitable for its new condition. It will be forced to buy modern weapons and to seek training for its officers in modern surroundings. Similarly, in administration it may relax the standards which prevailed during the colonial period, but it will not go back to earlier practices. In its wish to appear as a modern state in international company, it will press on with the training of its officials in procedures recognized as obligatory in such diverse fields as public health and central banking. It may open many positions to political influence based upon tribal, caste, or party machine considerations, but it will be under pressure to keep the upper reaches of its administration sufficiently modern to join in the discourse at international conferences—of which new states attend a great many.

The most obvious field, however, in which colonial influence may prove decisive is the economic. Most countries subject to European control in the nineteenth and twentieth centuries became parts of the pattern of international trade. If they had previously been accustomed to subsistence agriculture and petty trafficking, they found sectors of their economies transformed by participation in trade in such products as tea, rubber, cotton, sugar, cocoa, and minerals; some had their economies overturned by the exploitation of oil. Not to continue with the production of these commodities after independence would be to destroy the country's capacity to import the capital and consumer goods which its people have come to demand in the period of colonial control. In some cases, such as rubber, it may be possible to find local entrepreneurs who can carry on the businesses started by Europeans; in others such as oil and copper, this may be impossible. Some continuance of former connexions is therefore to be expected. In some cases it is strengthened by the fact that the markets on which these local industries depend can be found only in the former imperial state. This is particularly so with former French possessions, the economies of which were firmly tied into the French protective system. Algeria may redistribute the land on which grapes are grown after the *colons* leave, but it cannot sell the bulk of the wine anywhere but in France.

Thus each Third World state is a hybrid in its equipment for international activity: it proceeds from a social base which may or may not have been greatly affected by European influence and example, but its economic and social aims owe a great deal to European influence. Its government wants economic development, which means, in practice, growing more like the economies of Europe and North America; it wants increased trade so that it can gain income and import more; many of its articulate spokesmen demand advances in education, health, the status of women, and the conditions of labour, such as are immediately traceable to colonial roots. These points are as true of the Third World states of long independence, such as Iran and Ethiopia, as of the new ones like Zambia and Senegal. The main difference between the two groups does not lie in their acceptance or rejection of objectives of a European type, but in the form in which their national aims are expressed. For the older, traditional states, the form is usually that of the expression of national authority by a monarch; for the new states it has conventionally been that of a national will supposed to be expressed through a national movement with a recognized leader.

National movements

National movements have been the outcome of foreign control. They vary greatly: any typology of them is likely to be upset by changes of course and propaganda. Their essence, however, has been the claim of an organized group to the territory occupied by the imperial power. Asian and African national movements have had much in common with those of Europe, but the similarities should not be allowed to obscure the fact that, whereas classical European nationalism of the nineteenth century was essentially *linguistic*, that of Asia and Africa has been essentially *administrative*. Both showed a similar stimulation of feeling against the imperial power, but there is a contrast between the strong emphasis of the former on local culture and social forms, and of the latter on the taking over of an administrative machine and existing frontiers. Both had racial overtones, but these were more particularized in the European case: it is no accident that the Irish were stronger in denunciation of the English for being English than any of Britain's later dependent peoples. The emphasis on taking over an administration rather than replacing one race by another was affected, in many Asian and African cases, by the existence of a number of separate communities within the territory which the national movement was claiming. Sometimes a single major group might define the national movement as encompassing only itself, but more often there was an attempt to override racial, religious, and other differences by stressing common cause against the overlords, and claiming the whole territory as sufficient in itself. It is significant that irredentism, an endemic disease of nineteenth-century European nationalism, has been fairly infrequent amongst the new Asian and African states.

Comprehensive nationalism of the kind described has been the most prevalent amongst the new states, but it has not been the only sort. In some cases a supplementary nationalism has appeared, directed against neighbours or other forces in the vicinity. The most obvious case is that of Pakistan, where resistance to Hinduism displaced resistance to British rule as the motive force of Muslim demands. Filipino nationalism probably owes more to resentment at Japanese cruelty than to feeling against the United States, which was the imperial power. Egyptian nationalism, nourished by resistance to Britain, has had its flowering in opposition to Israel. Such nationalism as exists amongst the Malays owes much to anti-Chinese feeling: while the ruling Alliance in Malaysia continues to include a Chinese element, the main force behind it is often Malay resentment of the Chinese.

Whichever way these national movements have gone in gaining support for the displacement of foreign domination, all have been faced, on gaining power, with the problem of legitimacy. It has been necessary to preserve momentum and support. The problem is universal throughout the new states of the Third World, although it has presented itself in rather different ways and along different time-scales to them. For some régimes the collapse of legitimacy was sudden: in both Pakistan and the Congo, for example, the first beneficiaries of power soon found that they could not keep it. In others, such as Burma and the Sudan, there was a see-saw movement of acceptance and rejection of those who originally took over. In Nigeria and Ghana a relatively long time elapsed before there was a collapse. In India and Ceylon something recognizable as the original national movement is still in control.

Various solutions have emerged in the attempt to retain

legitimacy. Examples of four will show how varied are the political conditions of the new states. The first is the combination of tight coercive control with indigenous symbols of authority, the classical method in authoritartian monarchies such as Ethiopia and Afghanistan. In Cambodia and Saudi Arabia this solution has been successful so far; in Morocco it has shown its power to withstand assaults, although it was a failure in Egypt under King Farouk. The second is the combination of tight control with a local modernizing leader. The main example is Egypt under President Nasser. The third is a variant of the second, often to be found in states in which the conditions for tight efficient control do not exist, but in which a mesmeric leader imposes his personality for a time upon those around him: Ghana under President Nkrumah and Indonesia under President Sukarno would fit into this category, especially if one considers to be characteristic of it a habit on the part of the leader of blaming external enemies for the country's internal troubles. The fourth is a system of loose control with intermittent severity, perhaps with a notable leader to provide unifying direction. India under Mr Nehru, Tanzania under President Nyerere, and Tunisia under President Bourguiba are examples. Ceylon is a case of this form persisting without the leader.

None of these is a reliable solution. Each may be upset by bad luck, external pressures, or internal disturbances. One has only to think of the radical changes which Nigeria, Indonesia, and Ghana have undergone to see how unwise it is to regard any solution as either perfect or specially suited to a particular country. There is no finality about régimes in new states; most of what is said about them by supporters and opponents is simply rationalization of the speaker's prejudices, not effective analysis of what is actually the case. The same is true of national movements. A 'movement' is, by definition, something looser, less formal, and more changeable than a party or a government. In practice, national movements ebb and flow unpredictably, and may have lost tomorrow most of the coherence which they seemed to have yesterday. Legitimacy based on the triumph of a national movement is thus based on shifting ground.

Local pressures

It will be seen that, although there is much variety in these solutions to the problem of legitimacy, each contains a large element of coercion. New and old countries in the Third World are all hard to govern: their problems are great, their ways are not settled, their sense of rapid movement in society and in the world at large is often considerable at the level of government itself, however serenely the life of the peasant in the fields may proceed. Those people who can get their hands on the levers of power do not give them up easily. Typical government is not a matter of a popular leader interpreting a general will; it is much more a matter of opportunism by the elements in a decaying national movement, coupled with pressure from other sections which prove to be indispensable or irremovable. As the states of Africa and Asia proceed, it becomes clear that two groups in particular are indispensable. One is the group of European-educated people in commercial, professional, and administrative posts, who take over from the colonialists and are the only ones who know the details of the government and the economy. The other is the army, which has often proved to be the only element combining discipline, modernization, and opportunity to coerce. It has become a sort of natural residuary legatee of power at the highest levels in Egypt, Nigeria, Burma, Ghana, Pakistan, Indonesia, and other important states.

If there is a common pattern for states in the Third

World, in spite of their great differences in size and wealth, it runs something like this. The economy is connected with the outside by the forces of trade and investment established in the colonial period, but the new government is not content with these; it wishes to add to them in ways that will improve the general welfare. Traditionalist states act increasingly in this respect like new ones. The society has a large peasant or tribal base, but this is unimportant in the making of national policy, except when the people have been stirred by some local fanaticism, often religious in character. The keys to political control lie in the hands of politicians, administrators, and soldiers, who may or may not be able to agree on broad aims, but who will certainly be divided into factions; of these, a military faction may have the best chance of coming out on top. There may also be the remains of a national movement, impregnated with myth but uncertain of the way to turn. Its politicians began as agitators. Even where they had some experience of governmental processes, as in some of the West African states before independence, the situation which they inherit is inherently unstable. Their demands for independence have usually been made in terms which promise great changes when the imperial yoke is removed; these changes can hardly ever be made in the form in which they have been promised. A new state's social relationships are necessarily disturbed by a transfer of power, through both the removal of the imperial arbiters and the rearrangement of status and function within the state. Internal tension may arise through rivalries between tribes or communities; economic growth is a problem which a new state finds hard to manage; relations with neighbours and with other states may force local crises. How is such a state likely to take to participation in the general state system?

Participation in the state system

Two aspects of a new state's international relations are obviously important, however it may be situated otherwise. They are its contacts with its neighbours and its connexions with the former imperial power.

Contacts with neighbours are often what matter most to new states, as to old ones. In the complex of states which arose from British withdrawal from the Indian subcontinent—India, Pakistan, and Ceylon—this aspect has preoccupied much of the energy of the foreign offices. In spite of India's wide sweep of other interests, relations with Pakistan have remained the most important single issue. Ceylon's treatment of Indian Tamils, with its local and international repercussions, has remained a major question for all governments. Concern for one's neighbours may arise from long contact and free movement of peoples and goods, as in this instance; it may also be sustained by some sense of common purpose and experience, as is propounded by the Arab leaders of the Middle East and the Maghreb. But none of these influences points irresistibly towards harmony and away from discord. The Arab states are sufficient warning of how much rivalry can be generated by a sense of a common past; the hostility and the dilemmas created for Malawi and Zambia by their economic connexions with Rhodesia show how unreliable is trade as a common bond.

Connexions with the former colonial power cover a wide spectrum for the new states. It is rare for contact to be fully broken, even where great bitterness has arisen: the Congo's continuing ties with Belgium, and Indonesia's 'on again, off again' relations with the Netherlands show that the many links which the modernization brought by the imperial power creates are hard to break in even the most extreme cases. Britain's failure to gain favour in the Egypt of President Nasser is one of the few cases of complete estrangement. At the other end of the spectrum are examples of full co-operation, as between France and Senegal and the Ivory Coast, or Britain and Malaya. Each former imperial power does its best to maximize its contacts with former dependencies, so as to preserve their sympathy towards its interests, and, if possible, to ensure that they take something of a similar line in international affairs. Much depends on the extent to which the new state must look to the imperial power for help in administration, economics, and the general management of its affairs. Most of the former French colonies in West and Central Africa have remained heavily dependent on France; but Guinea and Mali have been defiant in many contexts, and Algeria and Tunisia have been selective in the demands they have made on France.

The best generalization one can make about relations with the former imperial power is that existing connexions in such fields as trade and education make a minimum of friendly relations necessary; that in cases such as Chad, Malawi, and the Gambia, where continued help with the national budget is required by the new state, relations will be very close indeed; but that beyond these conditions there is a wide range of possibilities, depending upon the aims and personality of the national leader (a Sekou Touré is very different in his ambitions from a Hastings Banda or a Tunku Abdul Rahman), the intensity of the hostility which was generated during the campaign for independence, the economic needs of the country, the local estimate of national security, and the self-confidence of the régime.

Relations with neighbours and with the former overlord may often be enough to engage the full attention of new states. Ceylon, the Sudan, and the lesser Francophone states have not troubled themselves with much else. Relations with neighbours are also, of course, the normal preoccupations of the older traditional states, such as Iran, Thailand, and Turkey, which have not experienced domination. One might expect, therefore, that participation in the general state system would often be limited. But in practice two other elements enter into the picture for all states of the Third World. One of them is more characteristic of the new states but spreads by contact to the older; the second is difficult for any state to avoid.

The first is the formulation of attitudes and demands on the international level which express the nationalist myth as it has been nourished at home. These are to be summed up in the comprehensive term *anti-colonialism.* Each national movement of any vitality has felt the need to express on the world stage its opposition to colonialism at large, as well as to the particular form of colonialism to which it was subjected. India, the earliest and weightiest of the countries gaining independence after World War II, set the lead in this regard and has remained one of the most vocal states in the Third World in generalizing its opposition to colonialism and racial discrimination. It was joined in turn by other Asian states, by those of the Middle East and of Africa. An orthodoxy of condemnation of colonial rule quickly arose. Each new state, having benefited in its own achievement of independence by the international pressure set up by the anti-colonialism of those which had preceded it, joined in on behalf of those peoples still under domination. The older traditional states such as Ethiopia and Afghanistan joined in too. They became aware that their relations with the newer states would be jeopardized if they did not repeat the standard demands of anti-colonialism. In any case, they had suffered sufficient rebuffs from Europe, in diplomacy and public statements, to make them sympathetic to any general movement which discomfited the previously haughty European powers.

It is tempting to make some sort of correlation between anti-colonial uproar abroad and actual or potential uproar at home, in the case of those states, such as Indonesia under President Sukarno, Algeria under President Ben Bella, and Ghana under President Nkrumah, which have been the most militant in generalized anti-colonialism. It is often said that these leaders stepped up their anti-colonialism as their own domestic circumstances became more troublesome. But any correlation of this kind must be made with caution. Undoubtedly any leader will stress unattainable objectives abroad if they seem likely to obscure intractable conditions at home. But the three men in question were all opposed to colonialism in something like religious terms: they had generalized their own experiences to the point where it seemed a duty to pursue the anti-colonial ideal, whatever the consequences. Their downfall was, in each case, attributable to local difficulties rather than to the positions they had taken up abroad. The essential point about anti-colonialism in the context of the participation by Third World states in world politics is that it has become an indispensable piece of equipment, a set of formulae without which a state may not be accepted in other Third World company, and a form of language in which much Third World discourse must be carried on. Its ritual significance is high, its practical effect low. But it is essential if Third World states are to be accepted as such; it has something of the same importance as the Christianity which medieval princes had to profess at every point, and in terms of which the justification of their actions had always to be couched.

The second element affecting the participation of all Third World states in the general state system whether, they are new or not, is connexion with the major powers.

For those which were British and French dependencies, this has come about initially through the former imperial power; but the interval between independence and involvement with the United States and the Soviet Union—for some with China—has not been great. In certain cases the connexion has come about through sheer bad luck (as with Korea, lying in the path of the Russian and American armies); in others it has arisen from the 'vacuum' created by sudden collapse of the former imperial power (Indo-China and the Congo are examples); in others it has been the result of contiguity (Iran and Afghanistan cannot afford to ignore the Soviet Union); but in most cases it has occurred because the global policies of the United States and the Soviet Union demanded that they try to secure the goodwill of new states which might otherwise be lined up against them. On the American side, the fact that a new state seemed securely linked with Britain or France, each an American ally, has not been sufficient to quell American interest, except perhaps in such an unusual case as Malaya. Mostly, the United States has offered material aid to new states, especially in Africa. It also sought to involve some of them in alliances directed against Soviet Union or China. CENTO and SEATO are monuments to this determination, which has now been replaced by the search for a more flexible system of understandings and informal agreements. The Soviet Union has had fewer opportunities to offer alliances to new states, but it too has developed a system of material aid, and done its best to enlist Third World sympathy. China, the most recent major power to seek goodwill in the Third World, has pursued a course seemingly affected by changes in its relations with the Soviet Union. Third World states have found it especially difficult to live to themselves or confine themselves to relations with their neighbours, even when their governments have wanted to. Moreover, they have found it difficult to confine themselves to anti-colonialist orthodoxy as their main divergence from immediate concerns. The world-wide ambitions of the major powers have given them awkward choices, which have sometimes included opportunities (as in the case of Egypt, a state which has consistently attempted to exploit its balancing position), but have sometimes been the occasion of heart-breaking misfortunes. It is difficult to believe, for example, that Vietnam and Laos would have been worse off if they had not been subject to rivalry between major powers. In any case, it has been hard for new states to ignore the competition between these powers. Burma is one country which has opted out of such a connexion; but it is very much an exception.

Anti-colonialism and involvement with Great Powers provide many of the most highly publicized and emotional issues which the Third World has had to face. Participation in the general state system is, for the new states, a complicated business for which they may not be adequately prepared. As we have seen, their mixture of indigenous and European resources does not usually include experience of foreign affairs. Their national movements provide the justification for taking part in the general anti-colonialist drive. But relations with the Great Powers demand a formulation of national interests which may be difficult to make at speed; non-alignment, while almost as much a ritual incantation as anti-colonialism, does not provide answers to many of the issues which arise in practice; and relations with the former imperial power, while helpful to a limited extent, do not always satisfy local demands or provide the opportunities which seem to be needed.

Uncertainty and nationalism

In summing up the position, it is desirable to stress two further characteristics of their diplomacy and their outlook on the world.

The first is the essentially provisional, flexible, uncertain and, indeed, hand-to-mouth character of much of their policy-making. The older states have an advantage here: they have been in existence for a long time, their range of vision is usually limited, and they are accustomed to define their problems in particular terms and stick to tested policies. Afghanistan, for example, knows what to do about its neighbours and the major powers, and is not concerned with much else; Thailand also, while taking a wider view through its involvement with the United States, has a fairly limited range of problems and seems to have traditional answers to them. For many of the new states, on the other hand, both problems and answers are at once bigger and more shadowy. They are equipped with régimes which are often unstable and are aware of the fact; they are inexperienced in many directions, yet propelled to seek action in them, through the inclinations of their leaders and the pressure of other states; they have societies which are subject to rapid change, but which do not provide a firm causal connexion between social demands and government policy. A government may be deposed overnight, foreign policy may change radically, yet life may go on much as before. We should expect arbitrariness and confusion in much of the Third World's diplomacy, since it does not proceed from the same settled basis as we are accustomed to in Europe—though we should also remain aware that European countries can show similar changes of direction unrelated to any expressed consensus, as in President de Gaulle's successful change in France's policies towards Europe and the United States.

The second characteristic which needs stressing is that of nationalism in the new states after independence. Beforehand, their national movements have been negative in emphasis, calling for the downfall of the imperial régime and its replacement by a local one. The ills of the world are attributed to colonialism. This aspect of nationalism, as we have seen, is generalized in international terms once the new régime takes over. But there is also an important change to positive nationalism, in the sense that, after independence, the régime makes every effort to harness loyalty to the state machine and its achievements. In part, this is a matter of the new régime's seeking legitimacy. It is also a manifestation of the conviction of every national government that the people's will is best displayed in adherence to itself. The nationalism of a new state is what is sometimes called *state nationalism*: not the feeling of a people struggling to be free, but the effort of a government to perpetuate itself and its sense of what is right. The quality of pre-independence nationalism which was called 'administrative' above is relevant here: the previous demand for control of certain administrative machinery governing certain territory is transmuted, after independence, into an identification of the people's will with the perpetuation and enhancement of a particular entity in the form of a state. Some local properties may enter into the performance—religion, traditional rulers, dislike of neighbours, resistance to local minorities, and the like—but the fundamental nature of the performance is not changed: it is that of a demand that local people should support their local rulers, and a determination to make the state machine such a source of bounty as well as coercion that they will be glad to do so.

In this the Third World is at one with the conventional practice of the older world, in spite of its frequent emotional rejection of what is characteristic of that world. Third

World states are, in fact, very much like other states in many vital respects. This central fact of their adoption of practical nationalism as a working rule, and their constant effort to augment the resources of their governments, links them with the system of international discourse and diplomacy which the European powers invented before they began to lose their colonies. Just as there is no practical internationalism amongst the older powers, except in occasional alliances and in inoffensive fields such as meteorology and airline timetables which do not detract from national interests, so there is none amongst the Third World states, except to the extent that slogans enable them to gain general advantages without individual sacrifice.

2

Afro-Asian Politics at the UN and Elsewhere

THE most obvious examples of concerted Third World effort have been at the UN and in the international bodies specifically Afro-Asian in character, especially the predecessors and successors of the Bandung conference of 1955. In this chapter I consider what degree of unity has been shown at these, and what kind of politics amongst Afro-Asian states has been revealed.

The UN complex

At the UN, Afro-Asian representation has risen considerably since the organization was set up. Between 1947 and 1961, the Arab, Asian, and African states, taken together, increased from 25 to 47 per cent of UN membership. The biggest increase was amongst African states, which rose from 3 to 20 per cent. These increases contrast with slight reductions, over the same period, in both the Soviet bloc's proportionate representation and that of the West European states.[1] While the basic form of the UN has not changed—the Security Council still has broad responsibility for enforcement, and the major powers retain their vetoes—its tone and purposes have altered with the increase in the number of Afro-Asian states. It is not now mainly concerned with security, as its makers ex-

[1] Hayward R. Alker, Jr. and Bruce M. Russett, *World Politics in the General Assembly* (1965), p. 245.

pected, but with issues of colonialism and economic development. These absorb a great deal of its time. Sometimes they merge with issues of security and of tension between the major powers, as in the instances of Suez and the Congo. However, it is only rarely that the Afro-Asian states are united in their UN activities. They are divided between Arab, African, and Asian-African groups, each of which meets regularly to discuss the issues before the General Assembly and tries to preserve some common strategy in voting; the first and second of these have overlapping membership, and form parts of the third. The Arab group is the most successful at retaining formal unity, with a record of something like 90 per cent of votes at which the members did not vote on opposite sides. The African group has fluctuated in agreement, but preserves something like 60 per cent of such votes. Asians and Africans together make a poor showing if one is looking for identical voting, which happens in only one vote in three, but manage to keep to something like 75 per cent of votes at which they do not vote on opposite sides.[2]

The discipline preserved by the Arab states may be explained by the importance of the Palestine issue at the UN, and by the existence of the Arab League, which tries to preserve a common front on issues affecting the Middle East. It is no index of harmony between them; over the period in which they have shown such cohesion at the UN, they have frequently been in conflict on vital questions affecting their own legitimacy. Their solidarity on Palestine questions at the UN has not extended to agreement over the policies to be pursued amongst themselves

[2] These rough figures are drawn from Thomas Hovet, Jr., *Bloc Politics in the United Nations* (1960), pp. 62 and 87, and *Africa in the United Nations* (1963), pp. 117, 141, 143. The clumsy references to states not voting on opposite sides are meant to draw attention to the reluctance of Third World states to vote against one another, and their use of abstention wherever this is an alternative.

on the Palestine refugees, the Jordan waters, and military action against Israel. The African states, which have had similar disagreements over the Congo and Algerian issues, have not been so fortunate in preserving a public image of solidarity; their disagreements have been carried into the General Assembly itself, and have resulted in different attitudes to the UN's own activities in the Congo. The Asian states have no separate caucusing group. They have shown little capacity to agree, except where questions of colonialism were involved.

It has been easy enough for Third World countries to subscribe to rhetorical resolutions against Portugal and South Africa, and to assert the need for international action to stem hunger, illiteracy, and disease. Their difficulties have arisen in agreeing to common action when the major powers were directly interested, their own security was at risk, or their own people were involved through ethnic or religious ties. In such cases they have become like other states: preoccupied with their own interests, while anxious to preserve connexions which might be fruitful in other contexts. The typical case of a Third World state has been put by Dr Conor Cruise O'Brien:

Pakistan, say, likes, as a member of CENTO, to vote with the West, but is also sensitive to Afro-Asian opinion, particularly sensitive to opinion in Moslem countries and strong on self-determination (Kashmir). A Western canvasser can therefore safely count on Pakistan's vote in a direct East-West controversy (Cuba, Hungary) but must make separate calculations if relevant racial, religious or colonial factors are involved For example, in a 'colonialist' issue, where the 'Moslem' factor tells on the 'colonialist' side (Cyprus) or where the Kashmir issue comes into play (Goa), the West may reasonably expect Pakistan's support. On the other hand, on a straight racial issue (*apartheid*), or an issue where a Western power is, or has been, in conflict with Moslem populations (Suez,

Algeria, Tunisia, Israel), Pakistan will be indistinguishable from the most anti-colonialist Afro-Asians. On issues where both anti-colonialism and the cold war are involved—for example, the Soviet moves on the liquidation of colonialism—accurate prediction of a Pakistan vote becomes impossible. It is in such cases that experienced Western tacticians become fertile in procedural motions designed to get countries like Pakistan 'off the hook'—and safely on to the Western bank—while sparing them the humiliations and dangers which loom when an Asian country casts an obviously 'pro-colonialist' vote.[3]

Such a set of pressures on a government is commonplace amongst older states, and has become more so amongst the Third World states as their experience has increased. Those with aggressively militant régimes, such as Indonesia under President Sukarno or Ghana at times under President Nkrumah, may choose to denounce states which submit to such pressures, but are themselves equally subject to them in a less obvious way. Nevertheless, Afro-Asian states have found it useful to preserve a certain unity on particular issues on which their separate national interests can readily be reconciled. Questions of reforming the UN structure so as to give more weight to the Third World than was envisaged at San Francisco are obvious examples: it would be foolish for any Afro-Asian state to object to an Asian's becoming Secretary-General, or to the enlargement of the Security and Economic and Social Councils beyond their original narrow confines. On issues of colonialism, also, a natural alliance exists. But beyond fairly obvious limits, these states are concerned with their separate interests, not with an effort to achieve harmony at what might conceivably be their own disadvantage. The UN is a useful platform for them. They can be doctrinaire in a ritual fashion which shows their adherence to the cause of liberation, but also diplomatic in

[3] *To Katanga and Back: A UN Case History* (1962), p. 18.

ways which keep the major powers in play and prevent the wholesale alienation of possible sources of advantage.

Much the same is true of other specialized agencies in the UN complex, such as the ILO, WHO, FAO, and UNESCO. These are now devices through which Third World needs are made known to the developed countries and are met within the limits of the resources which those are prepared to spare for multilateral aid. Taken together, they do not handle anything like the volume of aid provided by the major powers on a bilateral basis; but they do give the Afro-Asians (and, in this context, the Latin Americans) some joint say in the disposition of technical assistance.

The typical difficulties of Third World states in a UN context, as distinct from the more widely publicized advantages which they derive from the opportunities which the General Assembly provides for anti-colonial propaganda, are shown by ECAFE (the Economic Commission for Asia and the Far East). This was the first UN body in which Third World states had a significant say; but, although it was set up in 1947 to deal with specifically Asian problems, at first the independent Asian members were outnumbered by non-Asians, including the United States, Britain, France, the Netherlands, and the Soviet Union. The ambitious hopes of many Asian delegates for an economic plan which would do for Asia what the Marshall Plan was doing for Europe were nullified by the reluctance of the United States to risk money in Asia, the preoccupation of Britain and France with their colonial problems, and the constant political disputes between the Soviet Union and the Western powers. The Soviet Union, while anxious to score points against the Western countries and to support the Asian countries' proposals for increased trade and quicker industrialization, had little to offer in the way of concrete advantage. After nearly ten years of abortive plans and frequent recriminations, ECAFE began to benefit from greater American interest and a general recognition that its future ought to be a matter for its Asian members, not for outsiders. But such a change by no means solved its problems.

In part these arose from the separate interests of the non-Asian members, who naturally looked at Asian economic development in terms first of their own interests and afterwards of the possibilities of economic co-operation inherent in the Asian situation. Britain's view was confined to its own colonies and Commonwealth partners; France could look no farther than Indo-China; the United States was largely concerned with those territories in which it had a special strategic interest, such as South Korea, South Vietnam, and Taiwan. Only for projects which did not cut across their interests were these powers likely to provide funds and encouragement.

Such projects, however, were what the Asian members found hard to agree on. The smaller states in ECAFE were sometimes openly hostile towards Indian hegemony (much of ECAFE's staff has been Indian from the beginning); when Japan joined, the fear of some kind of 'Big Brother' relationship in trade, which would benefit these large states but not the smaller ones, sufficed to prevent progress towards increased regional trade. Schemes for industrialization seemed likely to benefit those already embarked on it at the expense of those inexperienced in it. Up till now, divisions of this kind have stultified much of ECAFE's efforts, in spite of the ritual tributes paid at its annual meetings. It is clear that, in Asian terms, there is no single policy which will benefit Asian states equally. Moreover, the trade and payments problems of Asian countries cannot yet be solved by increased economic activity amongst themselves: their economies must sell to more advanced states if their present industries are to yield satisfactory returns, and they must buy from more advanced states if they are to have the capital equipment which they need for further development. With limited supplies of aid from the developed countries, Asian states are essentially in a condition of competition, not co-operation, with one another.[4]

UNCTAD

The United Nations Conference on Trade and Development of 1964 (UNCTAD) represented an effort to break out of this dispiriting economic situation in which so many Third World states find themselves. It was noteworthy as being the first time that the Third World states as here interpreted, and those of Latin America, had made common cause in an attempt to get the more advanced countries to agree on principles which would improve their position. Some 75 or 77 Afro-Asian-Latin American states formed a common front throughout the conference; against them were arrayed an incongruous and unwilling company of developed countries, including the United States, Western Europe, the Soviet Union, and Japan. These were in no sense united, but they were in something of the same position; they were all being asked to improve things for the underdeveloped countries by altering their trade, tariff, and financial practices, and by making sacrifices.

The essence of the Third World contention was that underdeveloped countries were under a permanent handicap. It was stated that their export earnings were continually dropping in comparison with those of industrialized countries; at the same time it was argued that, if they were to finance their development requirements in

[4] Mention should be made of two constructive projects instituted by ECAFE, the Mekong Project and the Asian Highway. Both are going ahead slowly, in spite of political difficulties.

what the UN had already designated the 'development decade', their export earnings would have to rise. Whether these points were true of all of the Third World countries all of the time, and whether they imposed any obligation on the industrialized countries, are questions which the Third World negotiators took for granted. In their view, the developed countries should agree to radical changes if they were to live up to their frequently stated belief in development for the underdeveloped. The Western powers, especially the United States, showed themselves ill prepared to meet such demands as the '75' made. American thinking about foreign trade and its adjuncts runs along fairly well defined lines: freedom of entry for American goods; freedom of investment; generosity in technical assistance. Official American policy on world trade still follows much the same lines as laid down by Cordell Hull in the 1930s and 1940s. It has attained a chosen instrument in GATT, where the United States can bargain with countries to which it wishes to sell. But at UNCTAD this sort of bilateral bargaining against a background of assumptions about the worthiness of free trade was set aside by the developing countries. Instead, they called for a series of schemes to raise commodity prices, from which their export incomes largely flow; to provide preferences in the markets of developed countries for the products of the developing; to make financial aid a matter of compensation for income nationally lost by the developing countries through low prices; and to reduce the developing countries' external deficit on invisible trade.

None of these proposals was welcome to the United States. Some were more acceptable to Britain and France, although in both cases the importance of preserving preferential advantages enjoyed by their own associates (the Commonwealth and francophone states) induced some reserve. What the '75' were proposing, through Dr

Raúl Prebisch, was a built-in set of measures, a kind of trade thermostat, which would automatically improve the conditions of world economics for developing countries at the expense of those developed ones which were already their customers, benefactors, and debtors, or which (like the Soviet Union) might expect to enlarge these roles in the future. These measures would seem to involve considerable reorganization of the developed countries' existing practices, as well as formidable sums of money.

The Third World states were solid at UNCTAD; little has happened since, however, to provide them with what they asked for. Most activity has been in the field of commodity discussions. But the results by 1966 were still meagre. Commodities have to be attacked one by one; most (like, say, cocoa or copper) affect only a few of the developing countries; in each case the principal buyers are likely to put up stout resistance. General schemes for alleviating Third World difficulties seem as far away as ever.

Regional bodies

Given that Afro-Asian countries find difficulty in uniting on other than declaratory statements at the UN and its surrounding bodies, and that national interests continue to make themselves evident, we may ask whether a more harmonious spirit is shown at regional meetings of the Third World states themselves, without the presence of the major powers.

The first of such bodies to appear was the Asian Relations Conference, held in Delhi in March and April 1947, just before the partition of India. In many ways, this was typical of later developments in Third World politics. Africans were not present, but there were representatives of seventeen Asian states, either independent or soon to become so, and of certain Soviet republics. The topics included a number which were to dominate similar conferences in later years: national movements for freedom, migration and racial problems, and economic development. There was pronounced opposition to the continuance of European rule in Asia; the Indian, Indonesian, and Vietnamese independence movements were all eager to point the moral of their own experience. The conference was dominated in personal terms by Mr Nehru, who was to become the symbol of independence and anti-colonialism But, while there was a pronounced sentimental feeling for Asian unity, this did not survive the expression of general principles; there then emerged, 'more and more clearly, great mistrust of Indian and Chinese expansion in South-East Asia'.[5] The resolve to continue with such conferences did not survive the meeting at Delhi. No such conference has since been held, although the effects of Delhi were to be seen in collaboration between the main Asian countries (sometimes known as the Colombo powers) at the UN and elsewhere, and eventually in the Bandung Conference of 1955. However, no continuing institution resulted.

Lack of co-operation between Asian countries can be attributed to the great disparities between them in size, culture, language, and the like; to the different heritages of European colonialism; to the ambiguous presence of Communist China; and to the fact that parts of Asia, especially Vietnam and Korea, became the scenes of armed conflict in which the major powers were implicated. No one, in fact, has suggested a United Asia as an aim since 1945. But the idea of a united Arab nation is often brought forward. The Arab states have much in common, in terms of language, tradition, religion, and the Palestine

[5] Nicholas Mansergh, 'The Asian Conference 1947', in *The Commonwealth and the Nations* (1948), p. 107.

issue. Since 1945 they have had connexions through the Arab League. In spite of its original status as a British-backed body, this has remained an expression of Arab co-operation, and has attracted to it the newer Arab states of North Africa. It is not now solely a Middle East affair. As we saw, it has had some success in preserving cohesion at the UN. But it has not been able to stop the continual conflict between régimes in the Middle East, with vilification by radio and occasional resort to armed force. The conflicts between Egypt and Syria, Egypt and Saudi Arabia, Iraq and Jordan, and Egypt and Iraq, have made nonsense of the idea of Arab unity, plausible though it may seem. The difficulty has not been simply the over-dramatized struggle between traditionalist-monarchist and socialist-republican régimes. There is tension within the idea of Arab unity itself. Each state sees unity in its own image; that positive nationalism which was referred to in Chapter 1 shows itself in the Arab world in an identification of the right form of Arab unity with the régime which happens to be propagating it.

It is in Africa that regional bodies have appeared most recently and been most ambitious in their aims. In 1958, when there were only eight independent African states (exclusive of South Africa), the first Conference of Independent African States was held at Accra. It adopted a series of standard resolutions about non-alignment, territorial integrity, racial discrimination, economic co-operation, and the ending of colonialism. Two years later, however, with the advent of twelve new francophone states and the disruption of independence in the Congo, there was a split in the formal unity of Africa. By the beginning of 1961 there were two effective groupings, the Brazzaville and Casablanca. The first consisted of the more conservative francophone states, the second of the militant ones (Guinea and Mali), together with Ghana, the UAR, and Morocco, which attached itself to this grouping because of its opposition to the appearance of Mauritania as a separate state. Other states outside these two groups, notably Ethiopia, Liberia, Tunisia, and Nigeria, hoped to bring the two warring factions together at Monrovia in May 1961, but the attempt was a failure. By the following year, there were two bodies purporting to represent African unity, one based on Cairo and one on Lagos. They were merged in the Organization of African Unity (OAU) at Addis Ababa in May 1963. The OAU still exists. But it has found it impossible to agree on such matters as the Rhodesia question. Even on those emotional issues on which all African states might be expected to agree, such as the training of 'freedom fighters' for work in South Africa and the Portuguese territories, there has been bitter disagreement. To President Nkrumah's demands that the OAU should act as the nucleus of a single all-embracing African government, the OAU members responded with a careful reassertion of their own sovereignty, the inviolate quality of their boundaries, and their interest in co-operation rather than organic union.

The African states' difficulties are rather like those of Asia. We think of Africa as an entity because we see it so on the maps, and because we are accustomed to think of continents as entities. But this is not how history has treated them. No conqueror has ever ruled the whole of Africa or Asia; no common culture has ever spread throughout either of them. It is true that in Africa the plausibility of unity is increased by the spread of blackness south of the Sahara, and by the fact that the whole of this area was subdued by European colonialism. These facts generate emotional heat. But they do not solve problems: they do not create any automatic harmony in economic terms, do not solve the question of divergent languages and cultures, do not satisfy the immediate demands of local populations or the ambitions of rulers who have inherited administrations as going concerns and wish to put them to good account. United Africa is an understandable concept when one considers the need for dignity and status which formerly subject peoples feel. But it is no substitute for the solution of the particular problems which African régimes find in front of them.

Bandung, solidarity and non-alignment

It is fair to say that regional bodies encounter difficulties because their members' divergent interests take command of them, subordinating the common urges towards anti-colonialist unity except in cases in which no disadvantage to the state in question is likely. Is the same true of the larger bodies of the Third World? In particular, is it true of the Bandung Conference and its successors? Bandung was said to have created a 'Bandung spirit' of resolute opposition to colonialism and Western entanglements. Was this true, and has it been true of later developments? In trying to answer these questions we find ourselves moving into the sphere of Third World relations with the major powers.

Bandung's contemporary context was that of the recent conclusion of the SEATO agreement, opposed by India as interference in Asian affairs and a source of provocation to China. A further part was the existence of the Baghdad pact to which Turkey and Iraq were signatories. A final point of importance was that Bandung represented something of a début on the international stage for the Chinese Communist régime. It had been in power for only five years, it was not represented at the UN, and, although certain states had diplomatic relations with it and had been impressed by its performance in the Korean war, it was still something of a shrouded figure.

The tension between non-aligned and aligned states, and the presence of China, gave Bandung its distinctive character as a conference; the 'Bandung spirit' must be seen in relation to these two aspects. Much of the most vigorous debate took place on the issue of non-alignment. Mr Nehru attacked the very idea of alignment, generalizing his arguments to the point where any state in alliance with any other seemed in danger from his wrath, while any which was militarily linked to the West came in for special attack. Since one of his aims was to persuade the Chineses not to exert pressure on their neighbours out of a sense of self-preservation, he did not criticize the Chinese alliance with the Soviet Union. His demand for non-alignment as a principle of Asian virtue was vigorously denied by Turkey, Pakistan, the Philippines, and Iraq: the conference was almost equally divided on the issue. In the end, its communiqué gave little attention to this hotly contested matter, leaving states to make what arrangements they wished for their individual and collective defence, but enjoining them to abstain from 'the use of arrangements of collective defence to serve the particular interests of any of the big powers'. In fact, the communiqué was a highly constructive document which looked forward to many of the changes which have taken place since 1955, including greater attention to disarmament proposals, an improved status for Asian and African countries in the organization of the UN, and a wider system of international economic control, such as was later spelled out at UNCTAD. Its denunciation of colonialism was moderate.[6]

The principal effect of the conference, apart from the focusing of world interest on Third World possibilities, was in regard to China. Mr Chou En-lai's modest and con-

[6] The communiqué will be found in G. McT. Kahin, *The Asian-African Conference* (1956).

ciliatory behaviour, his evident wish to settle border and migration problems with other Asian states, and his refusal to be drawn into condemnation of even the most aligned fellow members of the conference, made a deep impression. The Chinese début was a success; it may well have convinced Mr Nehru and Mr Krishna Menon that the strategy of conciliation was right, and that China would not pose a threat to Indian security. Certainly, Indian opposition to SEATO did not slacken. Bandung also promoted closer relations between China and Egypt.

Bandung was an 'official' conference of governments which was widely regarded as a great success. It was expected to have been the first of a number of similar conferences, which its original sponsors were authorized to arrange. In fact, there has not yet been a 'second Bandung'. The reasons for this are instructive, and will emerge as we consider the growth of other Afro-Asian institutions since 1955.

First, it is desirable briefly to mention the formation of an 'unofficial' counterpart of Bandung, which has had numerous meetings. This is the Afro-Asian Peoples' Solidarity Organization, established in the last days of 1957, following a number of efforts derived ultimately from the Communist-directed World Peace Council. It was

> a kind of joint enterprise of the Communist powers and the Egyptian government, with the Communists bringing in their Asian and Nasser his Arab followers, and both sides pooling their contacts to build up African sections, while competing for influence over the independent neutralists.[7]

There have been numerous conferences of this body, much disfigured in recent years by disputes between Russian and Chinese factions; greater attention is paid to these in

[7] Richard Lowenthal, 'China', in Zbigniew Brzezinski, ed., *Africa and the Communist World* (1963), p. 154.

Chapter 4. The AAPSO's most recent manifestation has been its 'tricontinental conference' in Havana in January 1966, when it was decided that, while the AAPSO was to remain in existence, with its headquarters as before in Cairo, it was to be flanked by two other bodies with their headquarters in Havana, one comprising African, Asian, and Latin American components, and the other confined to Latin America and the Caribbean.[8] The function of the AAPSO, like that of the AAPO (All-African People's Organization), its African counterpart, has been to express the most militant line of anti-colonialism as expressed by so-called 'national movements'.

A further form of Third World politics were the two official conferences of non-aligned countries, at Belgrade in September 1961 and at Cairo in October 1964. These arose from special international circumstances. In effect, they were Bandungs without China and with the addition of Yugoslavia and Cuba. The split between China and India, arising in 1959 over Chinese incursions on Indian territory, and widening after the further armed clashes of 1962, provided India's main reason for agreeing to the holding of these conferences; China was automatically disqualified from membership, as was Pakistan. India thus had a better chance of pressing its own point of view amongst other Third World countries. It also suited Yugoslavia and the UAR to emphasize their non-alignment and to try to increase their influence in Third World quarters. But wider circumstances were also influential. The Belgrade conference met in the shadow of the resumption of nuclear testing by the Soviet Union, considerable tension over Berlin, and the failure of the Vienna meeting between President Kennedy and Mr Khrushchev in the previous May to settle differences between the Soviet Union and the United States. The issue of disarmament and of peace

[8] *The Economist*, 22 Jan. 1966, p. 299.

at large was thought sufficiently important for the conference to address itself directly to Moscow and Washington by letter and by emissary: Mr Nehru and President Nkrumah were sent to Moscow, and Presidents Sukarno and Keita to Washington. It may well be that the evident sincerity of much that was said at Belgrade contributed to later agreements on nuclear testing.

More important in the Third World context, however, was the start of a rift between India and Indonesia, which was to persist for another five years and to have considerable effect on Third World politics. At Belgrade President Sukarno of Indonesia gave full vent to his conception of the 'new emergent forces for freedom and justice, and the old forces of domination'.[9] He seemed to give complete priority to the continuance of the anti-colonial struggle. Nehru, on the other hand, dismissed colonial questions as things which, while important, were not foremost in the current situation in which the world might be going to its doom. Indeed, he likened detailed discussion of them to the debates of the League of Nations about the opium trade which he said he had heard at Geneva in 1938. This difference between concentration upon colonial struggle and concentration upon peaceful coexistence, a hall-mark of the arguments between China and the Soviet Union in the following years, was especially significant at Belgrade. Indonesia and India were increasingly to incline towards the sides of those two major powers.

The same rift was much more apparent at Cairo in 1964, where an even bigger group assembled: there had been 25 states at Belgrade and there were 42 at Cairo, the increase largely made up of newly independent black African countries. However, the upshot of the second conference

[9] From his opening address as given in Conference of Non-Aligned Countries, Belgrade, Sept. 1961, *The Conference of Heads of State or Government of Non-Aligned Countries* (1961).

was different from that of the first. There was not the same preoccupation with explosive European problems; the easing of relations between the Soviet Union and the USA was well under way. Again, whereas at Belgrade the Indian refusal to take up colonial causes in militant terms had rendered India unpopular with some African states, at Cairo the Indian position was stronger. Not only had China shown itself aggressive in Asian terms by its 1962 actions, which had been received with concern by other Asian states, but there had also been considerable Chinese penetration into a number of new African states. Moreover, the line of the 'new emergent forces' had now become much more directly identified with China, as had the diplomacy of Indonesia and, to a lesser extent, that of Pakistan. Cairo was, in fact, something of a tactical success for India, in that the states present gave their approval to the idea of peaceful coexistence while also denouncing colonialism in fairly detailed terms. Other states, such as Cyprus, the UAR, Somalia, and Cuba, got their rewards from specific mention of their grievances against the major powers.

The efforts to hold a 'second Bandung', which occurred abortively in 1965, have to be seen against the background of the two non-aligned conferences. Indeed, it had been a point of Chinese, Indonesian, and Pakistani policy, at a preparatory meeting at Djakarta in April 1964, that the second Bandung should be held *before* the Cairo Conference, because it was clear to them that more was to be gained in their several interests from an Afro-Asian meeting, at which all three could be represented, than at a non-aligned one, which only Indonesia could attend. India managed, however, to get the Afro-Asian conference postponed for a further twelve months, so that it would not be held before March 1965.

The moves to hold a 'second Bandung' had been made

in the first place by Indonesia, from June 1963 onwards. They had been given extra impetus by Mr Chou En-lai's visits to Asian and African countries between December 1963 and March 1964. He sought support for such a conference wherever he went. Some states (notably Ghana, Mali, Guinea, Ethiopia, and Somalia) were in favour; others preferred not to choose between an Afro-Asian and a non-aligned conference. It was already known that China was backing the one and India the other. It is not surprising, therefore, that there should have been much backing and filling about whether there was to be a 'second Bandung' at all; where it should be held; and who was to be invited to it. The preparatory conference in April 1964 settled the first issue but could not settle the other two, except to say that the conference should be in Africa. The OAU later decided it should be in Algiers.

The question of membership of the conference became the occasion of struggles arising from two divisions, that between China and the Soviet Union, and that between China and India. The two were intertwined, since India made common cause with the Soviet Union. For purposes of combating Chinese influence and stressing its own Euro-Asian character, the Soviet Union wished to be invited; India endorsed this claim. For purposes of demonstration against so-called 'neo-colonialism', China and Indonesia wished Malaysia to be excluded. India took the opposite view. In addition, China wished the conference to go on record in condemnation of American action in Vietnam, and was to be greatly annoyed by a statement put out in April 1965 by seventeen non-aligned countries, under the leadership of India and Yugoslavia, which failed to accuse the United States of responsibility in Vietnam. For a year or more before the conference was due to assemble in Algiers at the end of June 1965, there were running disputes over these issues in exchanges of propaganda between India, China, Pakistan, and Indonesia. Other states tended to keep quiet. There was a keen sense, amongst some of the more moderate African states in particular, that these quarrels were none of their business.

In the upshot, Algiers became a 'non-event' The immediate reason for its postponement was the deposition of President Ben Bella of Algeria on 19 June 1965, five days before the foreign ministers of the invited countries were to assemble to make final arrangements, and ten days before the conference itself was to begin. Nine francophone African states had decided not to attend before Ben Bella fell; soon afterwards, other states began to fall by the wayside. They either said they were not coming, or delayed the dispatch of their delegations. The confused reports from Algiers itself were one reason; soon, however, it became clear that states would have good reason to absent themselves, simply because of the intransigence being displayed by the Chinese, who insisted, in the face of the evident unwillingness of nearly all the potential participants to stand up and be counted on China's side, that if the conference were postponed it could only be because of imperialist plots. There were other cross-currents too. The Arab states were divided over whether to support the new Algerian régime in its demand that the conference continue, or give up the idea of a truncated and unrepresentative meeting. In the end the absence of black African states was the decisive point. Those five sub-Saharan states which had representatives at Algiers made it clear that, with more than twenty of their fellows absent, the conference could not be called Afro-Asian. The Chinese were left isolated; to save face, the ending of the conference was styled a postponement. But when the time came to prepare for the postponed meeting, China said it would attend only if there were agreement in advance to condemn American imperialism against Vietnam, cancel the proposed invitation to the UN Secretary-General, and not invite the Soviet Union. This was the last straw. When the Preparatory Committee showed no disposition to accept these conditions, China said it would not come. No conference took place.[10]

A future for Afro-Asian politics?

It seems likely that there is little future for Afro-Asianism as such. If we define it as the preservation of a bond derived from common experience of colonialism, involving a kind of overall harmony imposed by that experience, it can hardly be expected to survive the disappearance of European colonialism. States have more to do than to lament or glorify the past; their governments have more on their minds than the liberation of people who can be regarded, with some stretch of the imagination, as in a similar condition to that which they themselves were in before independence. For some of the states of the Third World, such as Iran and Thailand, it takes effort even to comprehend colonialism as an important issue. For others, which have experienced twenty years of independence, or have had a long period of practical autonomy before gaining sovereign status, the colonial issue may have become irrelevant through concentration upon more immediate issues. How, then, has so much enthusiasm for Afro-Asianism arisen?

It has come in part from conviction, in part from emulation, and in part from respect for the past. That is to say, the anti-colonial sentiment has been held firmly by some leaders, to whom it seemed the basic recipe for the world's ills; it has been emulated by others, because, although it

[10] For a fuller account, see T. B. Millar and J. D. B. Miller, 'Afro-Asian Disunity: Algiers, 1965', *Australian Outlook*, Dec. 1965.

was not directly relevant to their condition, it was clearly something which they ought to voice if they were to be preserved from attacks by their more militant fellows; and it has been continued by others through veneration for what they believed when they were young, or through sheer repetition of slogans which, while no longer applicable, were familiar. Each of these attitudes can be discerned at any general assembly of Third World leaders. Some, like Nkrumah, Ben Bella, and Sukarno, could find little meaning in the world at large except in anti-colonial terms. The whole philosophy of 'neo-colonialism', to which Nkrumah had attached himself before his downfall, was essentially an attempt to blame colonial influences for the problems which had appeared once formal colonialism was over. To leaders such as these, who were not prepared to adopt a thorough-going Marxism because of the constraints which it involved, but to whom a basically Marxist explanation of the world's ills was congenial, the attack on colonialism provided not only a view of the world but a solution to its problems. To Nehru, who began his public life with such a view, the cares of office brought a greater realism, but his speeches were larded till the end with intermittent references to colonialism as a comprehensive ill. To Sukarno, on the other hand, the importance of colonialism seemed to increase as his practical difficulties grew; his contrast between new emergent forces and those of the old order continually grew more extreme, with every difficulty of Indonesia, internal and external, blamed on the latter. The kind of attitude seen in its pathological state in Sukarno is, in some degree, part of the equipment of every leader of a new state.

There has been more to Afro-Asianism, however, than simply the personal inclinations of particular leaders. At every stage since World War II, it has been useful for those states embracing non-alignment to suggest that the

Third World as a whole was non-aligned by nature. This attitude, of which Nehru at Bandung was the exemplar, could be helpful because it suggested that alignment represented some kind of subversion of an abstract Afro-Asian ideal, however good might be the national reasons for a particular state's adopting it. The same was true of such extreme positions as Nkrumah's about African unity. He could hope that some people in all African states, while accepting the immediate problems of their own states as effectively inhibiting immediate unity, would still yearn for it in abstract terms; and he would gain some prestige as its apostle. The basic difficulty of militancy, however, is well illustrated by Nkrumah's own situation. While his militant gestures at international gatherings undoubtedly gained him an international audience, and rallied some of his own people in emotional support, they provided no key to the actual problems of his country—corruption, waste, an adverse balance of payments, acute antagonism between his immediate supporters and other influential groups. If anything, these problems were accentuated by the loudness and apparent emptiness of his pronouncements. The same was true of Sukarno. When both men fell from supreme control, the problems remained to be solved; the militancy seemed irrelevant to the tasks in hand.

In other cases, of which Nehru and Nasser are perhaps the best examples, a better balance was preserved between militancy and practicality. Nasser, in particular, has shown considerable flexibility in tailoring his policies to suit his and his country's needs: now modifying militancy in the face of hostility from a major power, now increasing it in the face of hostility from another. Well aware of the balance of forces in the world, and of Egypt's central position, he has shown more finesse than either Nkrumah or Sukarno. In all the cases in question, however, it seemed to the leaders that national interests would be served by what they were doing. The irruption of an intransigent China into the Afro-Asian context has meant a diminution of the stridency with which militancy could be expressed. Since the Algiers fiasco, extreme militancy in the Afro-Asian world has meant agreement with China. While this might be acceptable to President Sukarno, it is not acceptable to his successors in Indonesia, and is in fact acceptable to very few other Afro-Asian régimes. It is likely that Afro-Asian states will mostly refrain in future from committing themselves to meetings at which they are forced either to confirm or deny Chinese propositions. The risk of collision with the United States is too great.

Such a point enables us to see that Afro-Asianism might have a better chance of survival if it could operate without reference to the major powers, as a kind of self-contained, self-moving engine of international harmony. But that is impossible. Just as the existence of outside powers created the tension over non-alignment at Bandung, so the need to take account of major powers affects every contemporary attempt to be flamboyant in the expression of Afro-Asian interests. It is in a lower key than those struck by the Sukarnos and Nkrumahs that one finds the utility of joint Third World demands. Ever since the Asian Relations Conference of 1947, Afro-Asian meetings have been marked by a contrast between the grandiloquence of the leaders and the reasonableness of the statements in communiqués about economic and social objectives. Along with the expression of militancy at higher levels has gone the growth of a consensus amongst the professional diplomats and experts; these, like their counterparts in other states, look for concrete proposals which can attract general agreement. Their line of pressure on economic matters, culminating in UNCTAD, follows closely on what was proposed in 1947, allowing for the general growth in economic sophistication. And the practical efforts at self-help which Third World countries have adopted, such as common markets and Asian banks, follow closely on what the experts put in the communiqués at Delhi and Bandung.

We can see, then, two parallel lines of development in Afro-Asianism, one likely to disappear soon and the other likely to flourish. The first is the flamboyant militancy with which national movements equipped themselves when they turned their attention from national struggle to international involvement. The second is the practical enunciation of common demands which diplomats, civil servants, and other experts have worked out on the basis of their own practical experience and that of other states. The second is the more durable. The first has more fire behind it, however, and the ashes will take a good while to cool.

3

Third World and Major Powers

THERE is, as we have seen, no totally separate Third World, in any sense which would enable Afro-Asian countries to live to themselves without taking account of the major powers. There is a notional Third World separated from the major powers by the facts of history, and nourished in such unity as it has by interpretations of that history; but the major powers intrude at every point. Here I wish to examine their policies towards Third World countries, and to ask how relations may develop in future.

Looking at the major powers in the perspective of the Third World enables us to realize how greatly the bi-polar world of the 1950s has been modified by the spread of nuclear weapons and the incapacity of the powers to use these against one another or against anyone else. In the 1950s the debates at Bandung showed how tightly the notion of a bi-polar world, and of choice between the poles, had gripped the imagination of national leaders. Today this bi-polarity has become a thing of the past so far as its starkness and immediacy are concerned. Afro-Asians can still discern the existence of two broad groupings of states, Western and Communist, but are primarily aware of the divergencies within these groupings, the unlikelihood of open clash between them, and the consequent room for manoeuvre which this situation provides for astute diplomacy. The present position has arisen from twenty years of changing attitudes on the part of the major powers, corresponding to their changes in relations with one another.

Western powers

There are important differences of style and policy within each of the broad groupings. On the Western side, these have emerged most obviously over questions arising from colonialism. The United States was a non-colonial power (except for the Philippines), and has been consistently anxious to exploit the fact among Afro-Asians. Britain and France are ex-colonial powers whose contacts in the Third World are primarily with their ex-colonies. These differences have had a good deal to do with the styles adopted by these powers. The United States has shown more awareness of the potentialities of the Third World than the other two: it has taken much more notice of Third World opinion at the UN, stood behind numerous schemes for alleviating poverty and improving conditions in Africa and Asia, and devoted considerable diplomatic and scholastic resources to the further understanding of Third World affairs. At times it has expressed muted criticism of the colonial policies of fellow members of NATO, and it has tended to dissociate itself from these policies. Partly because of natural pride in their country's historical status as the first ex-colony of consequence, and partly because of their extreme sensitiveness to charges of 'neo-colonialism', Americans in positions of power have stressed opposition to continued colonial rule. Because the United States has only one ex-colony, it has taken a broader view of formerly colonial areas than either Britain or France.

These two powers have understandably concentrated on the countries they know best. In Britain's case this has meant emphasis on the Commonwealth as a unique association of ex-colonies with a former metropolitan power; in France's, consolidating links with the new states which speak French. The two styles are different, but the aim has been broadly the same: to capitalize upon previous connexions, and maintain advantages in trade and in consultation with the new sovereign states. The British system is looser than the French because the British colonial system was looser. But in each case there has been an assumption that the part of the Third World that mattered most was the part which spoke English or French. Such a view, unrelated to questions of global strategy, has not always suited the United States. Similarly, the fact that Britain and France have had to divest themselves of certain colonies while striving to maintain good relations with others now sovereign states, has given their outlook a relatively domestic character which the United States has been able to avoid. France, while still in the agony of the Algerian affair, had little chance to take a broad view of the Third World; Britain, struggling to end the Rhodesian imbroglio, can hardly take more than a defensive posture. These differences are reflected in the comparison between the American attitude to the UN on the one hand—expansive, co-operative, embodying a constant search for allies and associates; and the British and French on the other, essentially defensive and occasionally hostile.

If we look at the record of Western powers' policies towards four main areas of the Third World—the Middle East, South Asia, Southeast Asia, and Africa—these differences become clearer.

Most British and French policy in the Middle East since 1945 is epitomized by the Suez failure of 1956. Both countries were motivated by considerations that could reasonably be called colonialist. The British government, obsessed by the notion of Britain as a policeman in the area, in spite of failures in Palestine, Iraq, Egypt, and Jordan, transposed this colonialist urge into the key of world politics, and decided that President Nasser must be stopped before he became a Hitler. France was more directly concerned with the ownership of the Canal and with the impact of Egyptian propaganda in French North Africa. In the event, neither power gained its end; a major reason for their failure was the determination of the United States not to support them, in order not to be tarred with the colonialist brush. American policy has been tortuous and often unsuccessful, but has never suffered such a setback as Suez. The early hope of a Middle East defence organization which would bring the Arab states into an anti-Communist alliance soon faded. CENTO has been no substitute for it. The United States has persisted, however, in trying to make friends with Arab states, notwithstanding the heavy handicap of its attachment to Israel. Very substantial economic aid, especially of foodstuffs to Egypt, has brought this about. The cooling of tempers between the United States and the Soviet Union has also made it easier for American policy to achieve limited objectives.

In South Asia France has had no interest since M. Mendès France handed over Pondicherry to India. Britain's efforts to influence events have been surprisingly few, considering the long British involvement before 1947. But the Britain which gave up India, Ceylon, and Burma in 1947 was exhausted by war and preoccupied by domestic problems; by the time Britain could afford some sort of effort in India and Pakistan, it was clear that the economic troubles of those countries were so great that only the United States could have much effect on them, and that the Kashmir issue, for which Britain had been initially responsible, was one which it could no longer hope to settle. Attempts within the Commonwealth system to bring India and Pakistan closer have all been failures. Britain is still dogged by the consequences of partition in any attempt to suggest solutions. The United States, with no such handicap, has had to go carefully since India's opposition to SEATO was proclaimed by Mr Nehru. The Chinese attacks on India eventually modified the official

Indian view, but the United States is still the target of frequent attacks by Indian leftists, in and out of the Congress; any attempt to help India in military ways is immediately represented as a derogation of Indian freedom. Here again, however, the rapprochement between the United States and the Soviet Union has made the problem less acute.

It is in and around Southeast Asia that the three Western powers have had their most continuous experience of difficulties involving Third World states. The United States's refusal to recognize the Communist government of China, and its protection of Taiwan, counted for a time as a black mark with many Third World governments; this has become less of an issue in recent years, with China's change of face, but its effects linger. American protection of South Korea had something of the same effect. American military action in Vietnam has been serious and prolonged, but had not been so disastrous in its effect on Third World opinion if it had occurred before, say, China's attacks on India. While Afro-Asian countries have refused to give active support to the United States, some seem to have felt that, without American intervention, China might have gained further advantages through the spread of subservient Communist régimes in Southeast Asia. Such a view may be right or wrong; but it seems to have operated to still what would otherwise have been widespread anti-American clamour. Yet it is likely that the longer the war in Vietnam, and the more profound the destruction there, the less small Afro-Asian states will be prepared to accept American military intervention as a solution to their internal and border troubles. Britain and France, on the other hand, have concentrated on their ex-colonies in Southeast Asia, following their relinquishment of sovereignty in the 1950s. This concentration, more thorough with Britain because of confrontation between Malaysia and Indonesia, has been real enough but is illusory for the future: hardly anyone believes that either Britain or France will be a permanent factor in the politics of the area. The United States probably will be.

In Africa both Britain and France have been concerned almost exclusively with the decolonization process and with keeping good relations with ex-colonies. The United States, with no such problem, has concentrated upon the attempt to combat Russian and Chinese influence in the new states. Economic aid has been a principal weapon. Here again, American policy has been to dissociate itself from colonial associations and emphasize the sovereignty of the new states, while hinting that Communist connexions will produce no good result. The comparative balance between the major powers since most African states gained independence has meant that these states could largely pick and choose their sources of aid; but the fact that so many of them have proved suspicious of Russian and Chinese intentions has given the United States numerous opportunities.

Thus, of the Western powers, it is only the United States which has consistently pursued an overriding policy throughout the Third World, that of trying to reduce Communist influence, and, wherever possible, stemming Communist advance. The British and French have done this in particular cases where their colonial or ex-colonial commitments called for it, but their main interest has been in converting their former colonial systems into post-colonial systems which, while parts of international society, gave prime attention to British or French concerns. The British, with a vast, sprawling, and diverse empire to convert, have been less successful at this than the French, whose empire was more compact and more tightly bound to the metropolitan country in economic and cultural matters. Taking the three powers together, it cannot be said that they have pursued anything like a concerted Afro-Asian policy. Even when they have acted together, as in the formation of SEATO, they have quickly diverged over the lines to follow; and they were unable to find common ground over either Suez or the Congo.

Communist powers: the Soviet Union

The Western powers have no philosophy of international relations that can be applied directly to the Third World; their style and policies arise from their former experience and their sense of present needs. Communists, however, have such a philosophy—or its beginnings—and the activities of the two major Communist powers, the Soviet Union and China, are a fascinating mixture of dogma and necessity, as applied to relations with Third World countries. Since Lenin, in his *Imperialism*, put these countries into a setting agreeable to militants there, Communists have had the advantage of a doctrine which could be expected to strike a responsive chord in colonial peoples. From the Soviet and Chinese angle, it is clear gain that much intellectual opinion in Third World countries should assume the broad truth of what Lenin wrote about economic exploitation and revolutionary situations. The difficulty comes from the assumption that successful revolutions can only be led by Communists.

In the early days of Russian hopes for effective revolution in the colonial areas, in the 1920s and 1930s, the emphasis was on Communist parties controlled by the Comintern. Communist polemicists spent much time in discussing the strategy they should adopt. India and China were the two examples for debate; in both, the problem was to decide which political forces the Communists should join with, and whether such alliances were even desirable. The disastrous alliance with the Kuomintang, culminating in massacres of Communists in 1927, seemed to point in one direction, towards the rejection of bourgeois allies. The impossibility of the Indian Communists' gaining power except in collaboration with the Indian Congress seemed to point in the other. Nowhere could a Communist party gain significant influence on its own account, until the Chinese Communists, after their defeat, began to assert local control from their fastnesses in Yenan.

However theoretical this debate may have been in pre-war days, with most Third World countries firmly in the grip of European powers, it grew more practical in the post-war situation. Slowly the Russians and their associates were shown that Communist parties, while sometimes influential, could not materially affect the issues of independence. Movements like the Indian Congress, the Muslim League, the Anti-Fascist Peoples' Friendship League in Burma, and Colonel Nasser's Egyptian officers, were often affected by Marxist ideas and Communist contacts, but they were not under Communist control. Sometimes, on gaining power, they were in armed conflict with Communist parties and movements. In doctrinal terms, these successful movements, leading to national governments, were composed of the 'national bourgeoisie': they could be regarded as either 'progressive' or 'unprogressive', to the extent that they seemed to forward the emancipation of their peoples by an eventual Communist government. But this sort of government remained a pious wish. Only in China did the national bourgeoisie give up its hold, and there only after a cruel civil war. There was, however, another means of deciding whether the national governments were progressive, apart from their position as transmission belts towards 'socialism'. It was the extent to which they supported Soviet policies in the world at large. As in Europe, it has been the Soviet Union's custom to grade Third World governments in terms of their adherence to the policies which the Soviet Union itself puts forward to ensure the safety and prosperity of that bastion of socialism. Thus, while Mr Nehru's government continued to give implicit support to Britain's participation in NATO, it was an unprogressive one; when it turned to outright denunciation of military pacts it became progressive. In this way it was possible for the Soviet Union to select its favourites amongst Third World states, giving pride of place to those which not only rejected military alliances with the United States, but also denounced colonialism in militant terms and enlarged the state sector in their economies. In African terms, the palm was won by the Ghana–Guinea–Mali group: President Sekou Touré received a Lenin Prize in 1961, President Nkrumah one in 1962, and President Keita one in 1963. These countries even achieved the distinction of filling out a new category of Soviet dogma after 1960, that of 'national democratic states', in spite of their lack of Communist parties.[1] The downfall of President Nkrumah has presumably caused Ghana to disappear from this list, unless his successors take the same line as he did, in which case the character of the state will prove not to have changed.

The move in Soviet orthodoxy from endorsement of Communist parties as the only road to progress, to endorsement of national governments which follow policies agreeable to Soviet interests, has not been an easy one. Apart from the difficulty to Soviet leaders in persuading Third World leaders such as Nehru, Nasser, and Nkrumah that they

[1] See William T. Shinn, Jr., 'The "National Deomocratic State": A Communist Program for Less-Developed Areas', *World Politics*, Apr. 1963. For enlightening comment on the whole problem of definition, see Hugh Seton-Watson, 'The "National Bourgeoisie" in Soviet Strategy', in his *Nationalism and Communism* (1964).

should forget the insults heaped on them before they became progressive influences, there has been further trouble with China, which has seized on the issue of co-operation with national bourgeoisie to belabour the Russians for hypocrisy. The effect of China as a second pole of Communist activity in the Third World has been to complicate Soviet relations with Third World countries, but also to spur the Russians on to greater efforts: they now have two forms of influence to counteract, those of the western powers and of the Chinese.

In Africa the Soviet Union has often been able to combat with its trade and aid concessions the propaganda advantage the Chinese possess in being coloured people with a background of resistance to Western economic domination. While neither has much influence amongst the Brazzaville states, the Soviet Union has been longer in action in other parts of West Africa, especially in Ghana–Guinea–Mali, and has been able to render solid assistance to the local governments. However, it did not gain much kudos over either the Congo or Algerian imbroglios: the establishment of the Patrice Lumumba Friendship University in Moscow and verbal support for the Algerian rebels were no substitute for armed assistance in the eyes of many militants, and the role played by the Soviet Union in regard to the UN operations in the Congo was sufficiently ambiguous to warn African governments of the Soviet Union's primary concern for its own interests. There has also been considerable scepticism about Russian intentions in setting up special study centres in African countries and in bringing many young Africans to Moscow for study. Centres in Kenya and Ghana have been stigmatized as training grounds for local subversion. Students in the Soviet Union have been subjected to close political control and have also encountered racial discrimination on the social plane. Neither of these influences is strong enough to turn African states against Soviet policies if they find these congenial on other grounds; but they tarnish the Soviet image, as does the constant enmity between Soviet and Chinese representatives at militant conferences.

In South Asia Russian efforts have recently had their greatest single success with Third World governments: the Tashkent conference, at which the Soviet Union acted as host and honest broker to India and Pakistan in settling arrangements after their 1965 war. Soviet initiative in this matter was not deplored by the United States, which approved of the Soviet desire to meet the Chinese challenge in the area. Before the war began, the Soviet Union had been selling arms to India, and China had been verbally supporting the Pakistani case over Kashmir. From the Soviet viewpoint it was important to lose none of the goodwill which had been gained with India, while not antagonizing Pakistan. Both aims seem to have been accomplished. If the Soviet Union can appear reasonably impartial between these two quarrelsome states, it can hope to minimize Chinese influence while being widely regarded as the epitome of its much-publicised policy of 'peaceful coexistence'. The alternative is a highly tense situation near the borders of the Soviet Union itself.

In Southeast Asia Russian activity has been relatively slight in recent years, except in Indonesia, where again the Soviet Union was affected by the prospect that China would enlist President Sukarno's government as part of its own entourage. Indonesia was sold considerable quantities of Russian arms. In spite of the fact that payment has been slow, the Soviet Union can hope, following President Sukarno's eclipse, that the Indonesian army leaders will be grateful to the country which provided them with their equipment, especially since it was an open secret in Djakarta that the Soviet Union strongly disapproved of President Sukarno's identification of the 'new emergent forces' with China and those supporting it.

In the Middle East the Soviet Union has been constantly active since its immediate post-war pressure on Iran over Azerbaijan. Its policy has been almost as varied as those of Britain and the United States. The Middle East is an area of classic concern for Communists, and, being close to the borders of the Soviet Union, involves Russian interests directly. In strict terms, no Middle Eastern government is fully satisfactory from a Soviet point of view, whether it is royalist, Nasserist, on good or poor terms with the United States. Some régimes, especially the Turkish and Iranian, have been frequently under Soviet attack for their close connexion with the United States; this sensitivity has only recently begun to wane. One can discern a kind of longing amongst Soviet leaders for a properly progressive régime in the area. Such a desire broke surface in 1959, when General Kassem's régime in Iraq seemed for a time likely to come under Communist control, and was hailed by the Soviet Union in terms which immediately gave offence to President Nasser. But the Kassem government did not last. Neither did the breach between the Soviet Union and the UAR, which, in spite of its stern control of local Communists and its constant emphasis on nationalism as a vitalizing force, has generally received Soviet approval for its strong objections to Western bases in the Middle East, and its willingness to take the militant line on colonialism. Arms from Czechoslovakia enabled Egypt to break the tripartite Western ban on arms shipments to the Middle East in 1955; Soviet threats helped to isolate Britain, France, and Israel in the Suez affair of 1956; Soviet capital and techniques went to build the High Dam after the United States and Britain had decided not to advance the money; the Soviet Union has bought cotton at times when Egypt could not find buyers; and the Communist states of eastern Europe have traded with the UAR on terms which, while rarely satisfactory, have been preferable to the turmoil which would have resulted if the gap in the UAR's balance of payments had been left unchecked. Only over the issue of the treatment of Arab Communists has the Soviet Union earned condemnation from President Nasser.

Communist powers: China

The Chinese Communists are now more doctrinal than the Russians in their public statements, continually asserting that the Russians put coexistence with the United States before the encouragement of revolutionary struggle, and that they compromise with bourgeois Afro-Asian governments which might otherwise be swept away by the revolutionary storm. Yet there is little to choose between the two countries in performance. The Chinese leaders have not given armed support to any revolutionary movement; their use of war has been confined to their own borders. They have given rapturous welcomes in Peking to the ruler of Afghanistan, to Prince Sihanouk, and to President Ayub Khan. Mr Chou En-lai has been as attentive to President Nasser's wishes as any Russian leader. President Sukarno was acclaimed except when his régime was being unpleasant to the local Chinese. Clearly, both the Soviet Union and China fête those leaders who seem likely to agree with their policies, and attack those who do not; the nature of the régime is a secondary consideration. It is not in the ordinary business of international relations, but in the shadow-play of doctrinal conflict in the Communist world that China achieves the ferocity which it preaches.

Nevertheless, there is no reason to doubt that the

Chinese leaders dislike the pretensions of the Soviet Union and consider that they have a prior right to lead the Afro-Asian countries to socialism. China is, after all, the traditional exemplar of the evils of colonialism. Although no European power ever gained complete control of China, it was effectively tied to the economic aims of not one but a number of them, subjected to unequal treaties (including those with Russia), and laid open to attack by the Japanese. It is not the Ugandas and Burmas that appear in classic anti-colonial texts as examples of the evil to be wiped out, but China. When China took its place amongst Afro-Asian countries at Bandung in 1955, affable and accommodating, there was a certain appropriateness in the joining of hands between it and other victims of European depredation. The Chinese probably felt that the Afro-Asian world should be left to them to deal with. Not only were they non-European; they could also claim that the conditions of China were closer to those of most Third World countries than Russia's. It must have been galling to find the Russians assuming a right of precedence. If the Chinese had confined their quarrel with the Russians to forms of peaceful emulation, and had continued with their Bandung aspect, they would presumably have gained more acclaim in the Third World, and not suffered from Russian enmity. In fact, the impression made at Bandung has now been largely disrupted, through four things: the Chinese attack on India, the Chinese encouragement of revolutionary forces in Africa and Indonesia, the excesses of Chinese attacks on the Russians, and the insistence of Chinese demands for Afro-Asian acquiescence in Chinese policies.

The Sino-Indian conflict is many-sided in its effects; not all of them have been unfavourable to China. Some Third World governments were pleased to see India humbled, after so much assumption of leadership by its representatives at the UN, especially Mr Krishna Menon. They were glad to state their own versions of non-alignment when India looked for moral support against China. Asian non-aligned countries showed no readiness to blame China for what had happened, but sought solutions which displeased many Indian nationalists. But the general effect of the Chinese action was to reduce China's influence. It was so much in contrast with Mr Chou En-lai's posture at Bandung, and so inexplicable except in terms of Chinese arrogance or expansionism. It was recognized that states near China's borders, like Burma and Cambodia, might have to bow to Chinese demands, but this was not acceptable as a general principle to countries in which governments were emphasizing their territorial integrity and sovereignty. Further, China's action reversed the policy of mollification whch India had followed since before Bandung; India became a diplomatic enemy of China, with consequent shifts in Indian relations with the United States and the Soviet Union.

The Chinese encouragement of revolutionary forces in Africa and Indonesia, so noticeable from 1962 to 1965, has proved ineffective. In Africa it was especially noticeable in the small states of Burundi and the Congo (Brazzaville). Here the Chinese seemed to have temporary success in establishing themselves as benefactors and traders, and in keeping contact with Chinese-assisted rebels in the other Congo (Leopoldville). In Zanzibar Chinese influence seemed for a time paramount. But none of these bridgeheads has remained. Following the assassination of the President of Burundi in February 1965, Chinese officials were expelled. The Congo (Brazzaville) has remained friendly, but has not given up its connexions with France. Zanzibar has been merged with Tanganyika to form Tanzania, whose President, Dr Nyerere, while susceptible to Chinese arguments on certain issues, has maintained a balancing role not only between the West and the Communists, but also between China and the Soviet Union. Other African states have protested against what they regard as Chinese interference (notably the Ivory Coast, Upper Volta, and Niger), while Kenya and the post-coup régimes in Ghana and Nigeria have stigmatized the operations of the local Chinese embassy as subversive. It seems that Chinese over-confidence or impatience led to excessive zeal in the attempt to influence these countries. The same occurred in Indonesia, where the Chinese evidently overestimated the power of President Sukarno to control events, and were led into open support of the Communist party of Indonesia and of the local Chinese, with disastrous results after the abortive pro-Communist coup of September 1965. Many Third World states now have reservations about the value of Chinese friendship. In Asia China is an ever-present reality, with which relations are necessary whether they seem congenial or not; but in Africa, where a Chinese presence rests on no obvious basis of either established interests or massive aid, it is likely that more countries will disengage from anything but formal association.

Chinese attacks on the Russians have led not only to interminable wrangles at pre-existing Communist front bodies, such as the WFTU, the World Peace Council, and the World Federation of Democratic Youth, but also to a Chinese attempt to create new fronts with membership confined to Afro-Asians, and consequently with no weighting of votes on the side of the Soviet Union and its associated states in Eastern Europe. For journalists the Afro-Asian Journalists' Association, resulting from a conference in Djakarta in April 1963 with Chinese and Indonesian backing, was to replace the International Organization of Journalists. Similar bodies were set up for lawyers, youth, and scientists, and the Afro-Asian aspects of the World

Peace Council and the Afro-Asian writers' bureau were activated with Chinese and Indonesian control. The most notable clash took place at the conference of the AAPSO at Moshi in Tanganyika in February 1963, after which the Chinese actions just described took place. At Moshi the Chinese attack upon the Soviet Union's unsuitability to attend Afro-Asian discussions, and upon its selfish disregard for colonial peoples' freedom on account of its fear of war, reached a peak not previously witnessed. It was a shock to the Russians, because they could see that some of the delegates approved of the Chinese line, widely propagated in the corridors of the conference, that white men like the Russians had no place in progressive anti-colonialist movements. 'They sacrifice the truth', wrote a Russian journalist who had attended all the AAPSO and AAPO conferences, and was distressed at what he considered the deterioration at Moshi,

because they pretend that the liberation of Asia, Africa and Latin America is possible even without the participation of progressive organisations throughout the world, without those white people who because of their views actively fight against imperialism and its colonial attributes. There are in fact people with short memories who want to forget that the liberation of Africa would have been inconceivable without the Great October Socialist Revolution, without the existence of the powerful Socialist community, without the defeat of fascism in the Second World War, without the selfless struggle of the progressive forces inside the imperialist countries.[2]

It is unlikely that African militants did regard these matters as relevant to their own struggle. But it is also unlikely that they regarded the Chinese revolution as relevant to it; and the Chinese suffered something of the same penalty from Moshi and allied conferences as the Russians,

[2] V. Kudryavtsev, 'Problems of Afro-Asian Solidarity', *International Affairs* (Moscow), May 1963, p. 52.

i.e. a growing conviction amongst Africans that the Sino-Soviet clash was not their affair.

Problems of major powers

Each major power wishes to get as much support as it can from the Third World, and also to avoid trouble there. Each wishes to bring about changes, whether they are the minor changes that come from wooing a recalcitrant Mali back to the fold of France or the major ones which, we may assume, both Russia and China would like to see in the replacement of some bourgeois régimes by Communists aligned towards themselves. It is, however, important to recognize the difference between an approach to the Third World as a whole, and an approach to particular problems involving particular countries. Each major power would say that it had both; and in propaganda statements it would probably assert or imply that it was passionately devoted to the raising of the standards of Afro-Asian countries and their further development in freedom. At the UN, in particular, there is ample opportunity for this kind of statement. Many of the debates encourage it. Many of the votes taken are calculated largely in terms of their general propaganda effect. The concurrence of all major powers in declaratory resolutions, sponsored by Third World countries, and devoted to matters such as racial discrimination, show that the major powers wish to establish themselves as agreeing with, or at least not opposing, the concerted views of the Third World. In fact, however, these declaratory statements have little or no effect. They are recognized by all who support them as a form of international convention, harmless but necessary. From the Third World side they are necessary because they show local militants that their governments are pressing on with the fight. From the major powers' side they may have a similar effect; there are militants to be appeased in the West and also in the Communist states. But the main force of relations between major powers and Third World countries lies in the bilateral and group relations which, from the standpoint of particular major powers, can serve their interests best.

Recognizing this enables us to understand why Western powers cultivate régimes which are highly undemocratic, while Communist powers cultivate many which are strongly anti-Communist in their domestic politics. On the Western side the principal aim of the United States has been to contain Communism: this has been pursued by means of alliances and later by judicious use of economic aid, along with the occasional efforts of the CIA. Britain and France have had more modest aims; while agreeing that a general spread of Communism would be undesirable, they have been mainly concerned to see that the régimes which emerged from their former dependencies should continue to deal with them on favourable terms. It has been customary, for reasons of brevity, to say that these states had 'a Middle East policy' or 'an African policy'; but the reality has been much more confused, with the Western powers responding instinctively to crises rather than following a course determined by long-term considerations. Only in the declaratory sphere have they worked out policies towards the Third World as a whole. That is understandable, since it is only in this sphere that the Third World can be comprehended for long. Even here, however, it is noticeable that Western powers' concern foı the Third World concept seems to have cooled somewhat since its high points in 1960–1, following the rapid increase in the number of independent African states. Whatever degree of solidarity the Afro-Asian countries then seemed likely to display has decreased in practice. Not only have the Third World states proved incapable of uniting for long on general or regional matters; they have also proved difficult to influence, because of their changes of régime and their generally volatile character. UNCTAD was a shock to Western countries, revealing their widely differing approaches in trade policy. Their response to it has been a series of holding actions, which has allowed the splits between Third World states to show themselves. There has been no serious attempt to embrace the principles which UNCTAD tried to introduce.

The Communist powers begin from a standpoint of doctrine which puts the Third World into perspective as an area of opportunity, in which historical forces may be expected to further the interests of the Communists if given the kind of help which every generation is supposed to give the historical process. But it is clear from their actions that the prime reason for Chinese and Russian policies is not a carefully plotted course of helping history along, but a series of reactions to external events, coupled with an acute distrust of one another. I am not suggesting that in this, any more than in other spheres of action, Communist leaders consciously abandon Communist doctrine; it is rather that the doctrine is so imprecise, and the sense of national security so pressing, that doctrine is interpreted to serve immediate purposes of safeguarding borders, encouraging trade, confounding opponents, and improving one's general negotiating position.

The fact of nuclear proliferation has given clarity and precision to the differences between the major powers, by preventing them from effectively using force on one another (thus enabling each to become more individual in its policy), but also by making the use of force by any state a dangerous affair. An important result of the situation, from the standpoint of Third World states, is that, since the Suez failure of 1956, the idea of actively coercing

Third World countries seems to have been covertly dropped by all the major powers, except perhaps China. They now prefer to exert influence in less direct ways. The threat of force was, in any case, a diminishing weapon, because of the fear that in a bi-polar world the quarrel would become transferred to the two super-powers. Now that nuclear capability is more widely shared, and multi-polarity steadily becomes more evident, the need for force seems to have disappeared, except where there is either a direct confrontation between major powers (in which case the threat is made only to the other power) or a confrontation at one remove, in which what is held to be a satellite of the other major power is coerced as a warning. American action against North Vietnam is of the latter category, as perhaps was China's attack on India, which the Chinese seems to regard as, in some vague sense, an appendage of the West.

Third World states may thus feel that they have a greater area of choice in their association with major powers than when Mr Dulles was demanding that they stand up and be counted. But there are still cases in which the choice is slight. Small states with budget problems, like Gabon or the Gambia, may see no alternative to attachment to the former colonial power. States dependent on set forms of trade and investment may hesitate to cut the ties which bind them. States which have benefited greatly from a combination of trade, aid, training, and other benefits may not stray far from the former protector, as in the case of the Philippines. These are all cases in which a post-colonial situation is hard to bear except by reliance on the former colonial power. But the area of choice may also be affected by a state's geographical position, or its estimate of the hostility of those around it. States on the borders of major powers, like Iran, Burma, and Pakistan, have to face the prospect that if they defy these powers they run the risk of an explosion unless they secure guarantees from another power of equal strength. Iran chose to enlist American help against the Soviet Union; Burma has chosen to acquiesce in Chinese requests about the border, and to make no other commitments; Pakistan, having first aligned itself with the United States, has more recently come to terms with China, evidently confident that the danger of enmity towards itself is past, since China's enmity is firmly fixed on India. There was no obvious determinism about any of these choices, but each had to be made with a keen awareness of the risks which it involved; each was a matter of calculation in the face of actual or potential antagonism from a major power.

A further source of pressure from major powers, in contrast with that which comes from a border relationship, is the balancing aspect of Cold War politics, in which each contestant has steadily attempted to ensure that previously uncommitted states were enlisted on its side. Much of the attempted persuasion is secret, and the observer must try to estimate its impact from the behaviour of the states concerned. It is fairly clear that states such as the UAR, Cambodia, and Indonesia have been under the heaviest pressure from both sides in the Cold War, but have emerged (sometimes after internal upheaval) with a non-aligned position fairly well maintained. Their example shows that Third World states do not have to submit to pressure from the major powers if their governments are strong-willed; if they refuse, there is very little to be done against them, except the threat of stoppage of aid, which may either prove empty (if the state chooses to dispense with aid and publicize the fact), or have to be revoked in humiliating circumstances (which again reflects on the major power concerned). Cool-headed Afro-Asian countries have discovered how sensitive the major powers are to publicity given to their less creditable attempts at influence. The major powers, for their part, have found that there is little to be gained from attempts at coercion, in an era when effective coercion cannot be practised against Third World states, and other powers may be waiting to fill the gap if economic aid or military support is cut off.

There is, in fact, something of a pattern of relations which a Third World state may hope to have with major powers in the 1960s. It is exemplified particularly by the African states, which escaped the constricting arguments over alignment in the 1950s. In this set of relations a state may retain its old connexions with the former colonial power, building upon these as it wishes, without incurring much obloquy. The exceptions are states with very strong ideological biases, like Sukarno's Indonesia, and those which circumstances have caused to quarrel bitterly with the former metropolitan power, like the UAR and South Vietnam. The state may then pick its way through the attractions offered by the other major powers, maximizing its advantages through aid, and even retaining membership of aligned blocs such as SEATO and CENTO, without forfeiting the possible goodwill of the major power against which the bloc was originally organized: Pakistan and Iran have proved to be particularly adept at this latter tactic. It will meanwhile continue to stress its national identity, its solidarity with other Afro-Asian countries, and its wish to contribute to peaceful coexistence. Such a set of relations is possible because the major powers have moved from their earlier bi-polarity to a more complicated set of relationships, which permits small states to court more than one of them without suffering corresponding disadvantages.

Non-alignment, 1955 and 1966

We can gain some perspective of the opportunities of a Third World state within the sub-system of the major powers by comparing the situation of the mid-1960s with that of the mid-1950s, when the issue of alignment or non-alignment, as expressed in adherence to either the American or the Russian side, was being hotly debated amongst Asian and Middle East countries. As the debate emerged at Bandung, it was clear that the governments of some states were apprehensive of either Soviet pressure, pressure from neighbours, internal subversion, or a combination of these. States such as Iraq, Turkey, Thailand, the Philippines, and Pakistan sought shelter in alliances which, whatever their other components, were essentially alliances with the United States. Other states were either disturbed by the prospects of domination which alliances seemed to hold out, or worried by the consequences of strengthening the existing blocs. States such as India, Indonesia, and Egypt rejected the idea of alliance with the United States, and stated their position as that of non-alignment. In practice, this might mean some reliance on the Soviet bloc for arms and other forms of help; but it was not formal membership of an alliance, and so could qualify as non-alignment in comparison with the situation of the other group of states. Motives on both sides were mixed; it is a mistake to think that all non-aligned states (including India) were animated by the high-flown sentiments which Mr Nehru expressed at Bandung, or that all those which joined American alliances were there to serve the cause of freedom. But the essential point at the time was that the two super-powers, the sole possessors of nuclear capacity, seemed ready to confront one another, and smaller states, whether Asian or not, had to decide whether their interests were best served by joining the American bloc or by running the risk of either suffering Communist attack or being counted as Soviet auxiliaries if conflict did occur. In fact it did not.

The 1966 situation is quite different. Only a few states

(Burma, perhaps) would now endorse the full rhetoric of the non-aligned position at Bandung, and only a few (Thailand, Turkey perhaps) would take the opposite line. Non-alignment has become as much a distinctive mark of a Third World state as anti-colonialism. But in the decade since Bandung it has changed character. Whereas it could then look like a crusade, it now looks ordinary. Like any established ideology, it admits of wide variations. It is recognized as including the possibility of military agreements with former colonial powers, as Malaysia, Kenya, and some of the francophone states have concluded; it can also include all sorts of covert understandings with major powers, even with both the powers which polarized the world in 1955. The position of India is especially instructive. As the apostle of non-alignment in 1955, its position rested upon two assumptions: that it was not necessary to make a choice between the United States and the Soviet Union, and that China would act in a peace-loving manner. The first proved to be right, the second wrong. The first is still right, but the fact that the second was wrong made a great difference to India's public posture on the whole issue. In its propaganda it had expanded non-alignment beyond the practical question of whether to choose between the United States and the Soviet Union, into a kind of general philosophy of international relations; and so had some other countries then accustomed to follow an Indian lead. It was the general philosophy, rather than the practical question of choice, that was discredited by India's humiliation by Chinese arms. The initially vacuous Panchsheela was shown to be vacuous indeed. Non-alignment had seemed to offer a solution to the small state anxious to retain its separate existence and to preserve itself against interference by a major power; yet here was a major power interfering with the foremost of the smaller states. Moreover, the forms of protection which had been advocated by the *aligned* countries offered no obvious solution to the Chinese problem either. China was, in fact, a random element within the calculus which both alignment and non-alignment had seemed so carefully to provide. Slowly it became clear that the original polarization between the Soviet Union and the United States, however plausible in 1955, was not an accurate description of what the world was like in the 1960s. Not only was China a random element; France was one too, and both these powers possessed nuclear weapons. Whether the world was tri-polar, quadri-polar, or even quinque-polar, it was not bi-polar any more.

In some cases, however, the 1955 spirit remains. Some of the originally aligned states, of which Thailand is the most obvious example, saw the original polarization as between the United States and China, not the United States and the Soviet Union. For them, the situation has not changed, but has only become intensified. But for most Third World states, the issue has now become unreal, and non-alignment can be worn as a garland rather than a banner. Aid and trade seem more important than defence; and defence, in any case, has reasserted itself as more the basic problem of relations with one's neighbours than that of participation in a world-wide conflict between two super-powers. If the issue is still present in any force, it is in the area of direct Sino-American confrontation in Southeast Asia. South Vietnam is in the direct line of argument against non-alignment in the 1950s, Cambodia in that of the argument for it.

4

Interests and Groupings

I HAVE been saying that the growth of national interests amongst the Third World states has prevented the development of Afro-Asianism as a political creed, and has sapped the solidarity which militant leaders have demanded and Western opinion has often expected. But it can be objected that 'national interest' is a phrase short of content, and that it may mean no more than the sum of a state's actions. You see a state acting in a particular way, it might be objected, and you say that it is following its national interests. This implies that it has thought out its position in advance and is adhering to a plan of campaign. But there may be none of this to it at all; it may be acting through inadvertence or misunderstanding or impulse or sheer lack of thought. How can we say it has national interests when it may be only swinging in the wind?

It is true that clear statements of national interest are rarely made by national leaders, who usually prefer to leave themselves much freedom of action. It is also true that states do not usually stick to long-term plans in their foreign policies. But interests are neither policies nor plans; they correspond to that sense of direction which a man may feel when he knows broadly where he wants to go but is unaware of exactly how to get there. National interests are the concrete expression of a wish to do what is best for one's country. They are not immutable, but change with the persons formulating them; however, they always bear some relation to a state's actual circumstances.

For a Third World state, faced with the need to decide what is best to do in a complicated world, a set of national interests might be as follows; they are expressed as aspirations:

1. To maximize the prestige of the national government. This may well be of more importance to Third World governments than to those of more settled states. The new states in the Third World have régimes which rest upon a vaguely populist basis, and need frequent acclaim if they are to demonstrate their legitimacy. This can often come by way of visits from notables from other lands, state visits abroad which yield recognition from régimes which are widely respected, and bravura performances at the UN and other rostrums of propaganda value. The traditionalist states in the Third World have similar needs: the Emperor of Ethiopia and the Shah of Iran are well aware of the advantages of suitable display. Such an interest may well decide politicies in particular situations, and may take precedence over other interests which seem to the outsider more urgent.

2. To preserve sovereignty and territorial integrity. This is a truism when applied to any state, but its importance to new states with boundaries that do not correspond to natural borders is obvious. In some cases this particular interest may involve resistance to irredentist claims, such as those made by Pakistan over Kashmir and Somalia over the Somali areas of Kenya and Ethiopia. The issue of sovereignty is particularly important to weak states that need to provide their people with some concrete symbol of independence.

3. To improve the economy. Again this is a truism for all states, but may be more urgent for new régimes that have promised much than for those which are old and established. For Third World states, all of which subscribe to the imperative character of the need for develop-

ment, it is an obvious interest to pursue. In any case, an economy which is out of order because of calamities in its balance of payments may be a source of major internal discontent, as in Ghana and Indonesia before the downfall of President Nkrumah and the curbing of President Sukarno.

4. To be on good terms with neighbours. Most Third World states have difficulties on this score; relations with neighbours often form the most important area of foreign policy for them. It may be a matter of former connexion which has left scars and minorities, as with India, Pakistan, Burma, and Ceylon; or of long-standing animosities which impinge upon more recent arrangements, as with Thailand, Cambodia, and South Vietnam; or of joint economic institutions which do not seem to benefit all partners equally, as with Kenya, Uganda, and Tanganyika; or of the near presence of a major power; or of near-by states which harbour political refugees and encourage attempts at the overthrow of the given state's government, as in parts of West and Central Africa; or of abortive attempts at union which leave animosities behind, as in the Middle East; or of divergent régimes operating upon basically similar peoples and engendering rivalry, as in the Middle East and between Indonesia and Malaysia. Being 'on good terms' with neighbours may, of course, be interpreted in more than one way; Hitler probably said he wanted to be on good terms with the Austrians and Czechs when he took over their states. But whether these terms are sought by conquest, conflict, or co-operation, they are an obvious interest for new states.

5. To co-operate with like-minded states. Like-mindedness may take many forms, from client status with a major power to functional co-operation with a neighbouring weak state. It is rare to find a state that deliberately keeps itself to itself. The quest for connexion with others with similar views is almost universal, and especially

likely to be pursued amongst the Afro-Asians, where so many crusades are being carried on.

6. To be well thought of amongst Afro-Asian states. This is similar to, but not the same as, interest no. 5. A given Third World state will certainly not regard all other Third World states as like-minded. Some will be disqualified by other associations, some by remoteness and lack of likeness at large, some by differences of ideology, some because they seem obvious opponents on such grounds as irredentism or subversion. Yet it may still be desirable to associate with these unsatisfactory states on certain issues and at certain times because the wider interests of Afro-Asians or Arabs or Africans seem to demand it, or because it is considered that the given state will be cold-shouldered if it does not show enthusiasm for Afro-Asian causes. Militant states will sometimes interpret this interest in terms of moderation of their original proposals, conservative states in those of a more venturesome approach than they might make if they had only local considerations to take into account. The extent to which an Afro-Asian state values the opinion of other such states will vary from one to another, but it is fair to say that there is now a kind of minimum level of engagement in Afro-Asian (or solely African) affairs below which no state will wish to fall.

7. To avoid domination by a major power. Again this is a truism of states at large, especially small states, but its importance is considerable in the Third World. Nationalism is strong in Afro-Asian states, and is, as we have seen, centred upon the machinery, performance, and personnel of the national government. In such circumstances, an effective form of criticism, whether internal and external, may well be to say that the government is under the thumb of another. Such accusations are frequently made from the Communist side, when Communist powers see no im-

mediate likelihood of the government in question following their line. They may also come from other Third World states; the widespread detestation of Mr Tshombe as a national leader is a notable case. It is not only that such accusations may be serious; it is also that genuine feelings of national pride may be outraged by conditions which provoke them. Thus, even when a major power has become dominant, its client state will wish to avoid the appearance of domination.

8. To obtain assistance from major powers. This is the obverse of interest no. 7. Only the very exceptional Third World country tries to cut itself off from major powers altogether. The more normal method is to seek that kind of connexion which will maximize benefits while keeping the state dependent. Sometime this may be sought by pitting one major power against another in such fields as aid, as Afghanistan and the UAR seem successfully to have done; sometimes by attaching one's state firmly to a particular major power and repulsing others, as in the case of Thailand; sometimes by moving to and fro between major powers in order to emphasize one's own sovereignty, as Cambodia has tried to do. How successful a state will be depends upon its own skill in diplomacy and the degree of importance the major powers attach to it. Sometimes the assistance is solely economic, sometimes military; if it is military it will also encompass some economic assistance. The terms on which it is given will vary with the stress of circumstance. When Turkey looked for American protection against the Soviet Union, and the Truman Doctrine was enunciated to meet its need and that of Greece, the United States could largely call the tune in accordance with its own wishes. But in the case of the UAR, threatened by no one but Israel and quite capable of refusing aid if it seems to carry the wrong strings, calling the tune is more difficult.

Pursuing such interests, the government of a Third World state does what it can to maximize them without harming itself. In this it acts like any other sovereign state of which we have record. But, like other sovereign states, it is subject to a variety of pressures, which influence the extent to which it is able to keep a steady course. It is to be expected that the most important pressures will be external. We have seen how relations with the major powers influence the policies of Afro-Asian states; and we have also seen something of pressure from neighbours and from other Afro-Asians. All of these will influence the working out of national interests, sometimes accentuating an existing aspiration, sometimes blocking it completely. A pattern foreign secretary with a picture in his head of his country's vital interests could spend his whole time adjusting them to these pressures, and the pressures to one another.

But he must also keep in mind the pressures from within his own country. If he does not do so, his national leader will be sure to remind him of them. They include the personal ideologies of the leaders themselves (which can seem all-embracing, a substitute for all other considerations, in the case of an Nkrumah or a Sukarno); the leaders' need to maintain a position of strength and splendour in the eyes of their people; the need to fend off local opposition, especially if it comes from such quarters as business and the army, which are often in touch with their counterparts in other countries, and may have information and interests which do not suit the government; the existence within the community of minorities which may have links with, or enmities against, neighbouring countries; the local economic situation, which may call for special efforts to secure trade, aid, and investment, if local discontent is to be kept down; and the susceptibility of the local population to appeals over the heads of the leaders from other countries which can use such concepts as Arab unity, or African unity, or opposition to minorities in order to stir up trouble. Each of these is a domestic problem, in the sense that it happens at home, but it is also international, in that either the causes or the solutions lie outside the country. If internal discontent and disintegration become well advanced, as often happens in the unsettled conditions of many Third World countries, foreign policy may become volatile and uncertain. Indonesia in the latter days of President Sukarno's reign, and India during some of its periods of greatest uncertainty over Kashmir, seem to exemplify this point; at the other extreme, the settled internal conditions of Egypt and Thailand seem to have given their governments the opportunity to pursue purposeful foreign policies without the threat of local disturbance. The truly pathological cases of new states, such as the Congo after 1960 and South Vietnam after the downfall of the Diem government, show how internal instability can discredit a new state's attempts to get support abroad. Each Third World state, whether new or not, wants to avoid the combination of dissension at home and ostracism beyond. The competitive and declaratory character of much Afro-Asian joint effort, especially in Africa, brings these dangers nearer.

It should now be clear that, although each Third World state may be expected to pursue distinct national interests, the task of achieving these will be complicated by external and internal pressures. Internally, the pressures may be so strong, and may yet be capable of such change, as to alter a state's whole broad alignment. Apparently settled national interests may prove to have been merely the aims of a dominant group, and may be altered when a new group comes to the top. The example of Indonesia under President Sukarno has often been cited here, but may be mentioned again because of its dramatic character.

Indonesia was, in a sense, the pattern of revolutionary new states, just as India was the pattern of constitutional new states. Indonesia gained its independence only after prolonged armed conflict with the colonial power; India achieved it after prolonged negotiation. It could be argued (indeed, was argued consistently by President Sukarno) that the revolutionary character of Indonesia's fight for independence meant that struggle must characterize all its actions, must be a sort of emblem of Indonesian endeavour. This was a harmless assertion to his non-Communist associates, so long as it did not lead to advantages for the Indonesian Communist party or to international affiliations which they disliked. But when the President interpreted it in this way, and seemed to see the national interest as involving the closest connexion with China, North Vietnam, and North Korea, his formulation became unacceptable to the army and to many Muslims. His successors saw the national interest as the reverse of what he had propounded. A change of régime meant a change of direction. Whereas Sukarno had aimed at denunciation of the UN, connexion with China, and confrontation with Malaysia, his successors preferred to desert these 'interests', and concentrate upon economic links with Japan and an attempt to restore relations with Indonesia's close neighbours.

One can say, then, that there is no certainty about the line which any Third World state will follow, and that the future may see many vacillations in the policy pursued by particular states. Nevertheless, it seems certain that most will attempt to follow a set of interests broadly similar to those outlined above. In doing so, they are likely to fall into certain groupings, some similar to, and others different from, those which they have shown up to now. What is the future pattern of their relations likely to be?

Future groupings

In the first place, we may expect some continuation of regional groupings which already exist, and perhaps the creation of new ones. The OAU has not fulfilled the hopes of those who brought it to birth, but it is likely to remain as a forum for discussion, even if the quarrels between members truncate its total membership and prevent it from carrying out a broad programme of African liberation. The toughness of Portugal and South Africa, the weakness of resistance movements in those countries' territories, and the impracticability of mounting offensives against them in the face of opposition from major powers, are likely to cause a stalemate in Africa. If so, OAU can only be consultative in character, since African states will probably confine their practical co-operation to fields such as trade and communications. This means that the Union Africaine Malgache (UAM), which was supposed to be broken up as a political body when OAU was instituted, but persisted as an economic body, may prove an effective means of African co-operation. Whether any other than the francophone group of states can sustain prolonged co-operation is another matter. Even in the UAM group there are complaints about the effects of divergent size and comparative development, similar to those which have impeded co-operation between the former British territories in East Africa.

For reasons which have already been described, the Arab states may be expected to continue in their loose association, in spite of the disrespect which their régimes feel for one another. There are advantages to be gained from continuing the show of strength against Israel, even though there may be no intention of renewing general war. But the North African states (Morocco, Algeria, Tunisia, and perhaps the Sudan and Libya) may not wish to remain associated with the anti-Israel crusade, if this involves any sacrifice of benefits which they might otherwise gain. There is no obvious basic reason why they should remain as part of the mutually cannibalistic Middle Eastern circus, except that two of them (Libya and the Sudan) might be sensitive to Egyptian economic and military pressure, while the others are sufficiently distrustful of one another to prefer to be together in the Arab League, rather than individually outside it and subject to its abuse. Nevertheless, such an association of incompatibles is bound to attract the competing attentions of the major powers, especially the United States and the Soviet Union; and Arab co-operation may be at best a matter of convenience and declamation.

The change of direction in Indonesia might lead to a new regional grouping in Southeast Asia, the machinery for which, in the shape of ASA (Association of Southeast Asia) lies waiting to hand in Kuala Lumpur. The original membership of ASA was Malaya, Thailand, and the Philippines. It was thrown into disuse by the dispute between Malaysia and the Philippines over part of Sabah, and by the temporary association of the Philippines with Indonesia's denunciation of Malaysia. A rival scheme, Maphilindo, was put forward with Philippines and Indonesian approval as a means of consolidating 'Malay' interests in the area. ASA is more likely to suit the interests of a Malaysia in which the multi-racial, rather than the exclusively Malay, character of the country is being emphasized. It would also be capable of accommodating Singapore and Thailand, neither of which is Malay. But a Malaysian government which had decided to stress its Malay character and its suspicions of the Chinese might find the Maphilindo concept more useful. In neither case should we expect supra-nationalism of any significance; as in Africa, any future emphasis is likely to be on economic co-operation and cultural association, not on super-states. None of the regional groupings which we can envisage is likely to diminish the powers of the states composing it. Only if it guarantees their separate existence will it be undertaken.

Beyond these possible groupings of neighbours there is little chance of significant association amongst the Third World states. Their general tendencies are fissiparous; the very instability of so many leads not to a desire for integration with one another, as much Western argument might suggest it should, but to an even stronger assertion of nationalism, in the form of identification of the régime of the moment with the state's ultimate destiny. What future is there, then, in general Afro-Asian institutions?

If it is correct to say, as suggested earlier, that Afro-Asianism as such has no future, then there is no future for Afro-Asian institutions such as second or third Bandungs. Since the activity of these institutions is mainly hortatory and is concerned with colonialist and similar issues, they may cease to have any obvious utility once the newer states become fully established and only a few colonialist régimes remain. What will there be to talk about, except the economic difficulties of underdevelopment? Moreover, it is clear from the events of 1965, that some states may get their fingers burned at these assemblies, in the sense that they are called upon to subscribe to doctrines which they do not accept, or face the prospect of international abuse. The attempt to hold an Afro-Asian conference at Algiers was enthusiastically pursued by those states which had axes to grind, such as China and Indonesia, but only languidly by most others. Many were only too glad not to attend. The notion of general Afro-Asian institutions is much more attractive to that flamboyant militancy described in Chapter 2 than to the practical men who have to run the machinery of the new states; and the run of events is towards the latter rather than the former.

Yet there is certainly some advantage, to the practical men as well as the demagogues, in preserving a show of Afro-Asianism. If general Afro-Asian institutions seem unsuitable, the obvious alternatives are *ad hoc* assemblies such as non-aligned conferences, and the continuation of Afro-Asian consultation at the UN. Of these two possibilities, the second would seem to have more life in it. The professional diplomat, who will increasingly become the typical representative of Third World countries, is more at home at the UN than in assemblies of freedom movements. He is not being asked to work in a single dimension of his country's external situation, but in all of them: here are his neighbours, here are his enemies, here are the major powers, here are the other Afro-Asians, here are the Latin Americans as possible auxiliaries, here are the world-wide issues sufficiently enmeshed in the conventional machinery of the UN Charter to be manageable at the level of agreed resolutions, whatever may happen to them afterwards. A show of Afro-Asian solidarity under such circumstances can do no harm to the individual state's interests, and may serve them in many ways. But on an occasion confined to Afro-Asians, greater difficulties may arise: the compulsion of an anti-colonial ethic is stronger than in the more diffuse atmosphere of the UN, and may be used by this or that senior Afro-Asian country for its own propaganda purposes. Moreover, the UN does not contain China, the stumbling-block in recent Afro-Asian meetings. Non-aligned conferences do not contain China either; but they are highly susceptible to use in the interests of India or the UAR. The UN is a safer place.

Consideration of the groupings which might occur amongst Third World countries raises again the problem of militancy. International militancy is hard to define with precision. Yet, in recent years, Afro-Asian and Western diplomats alike were accustomed to regard Indonesia, Ghana, Algeria, Guinea, and Mali as making the running in attacks on neo-colonialism and in encouragement of anti-Western feelings amongst other Third World states, with the UAR assisting when its own interests seemed involved. These were the states which got applause from the Soviet Union and sometimes from China, which gave active support to the Afro-Asian Solidarity Movement, and which were most strident in support of 'liberation' movements. To them, and to the hesitant and intermittent support of India after its clash with China, Afro-Asianism owed its vitality as a going concern.

Changes of régime in Ghana, Algeria, and Indonesia suggest the end of militancy, at least for the time being. Guinea and Mali are insignificant states in their own right, small and poor; they cannot sustain an international movement without substantial help. The UAR, in spite of its constant involvement in African affairs, is basically an Arab state, and widely viewed as such. Its diplomacy is skilful and active at a number of levels, but it can hardly avoid giving the impression that its attitudes are conditioned by its own direct interests, especially in regard to other Arab states, to Israel, and to the balance between the USA and the Soviet Union. While India might still hope for something from non-aligned conferences, it will not seek occasions to face China in the company of other Afro-Asians. The failure of its neighbours to support it against China, especially at the Colombo Conference of December 1962, made India essentially defensive about the use its opponents might make of Afro-Asian meetings. If there were no continuing dispute between India any China, these might prove more attractive to other states. One Indian observer has even suggested that not only China, but India too, might be asked by 'the small and medium-sized Afro-Asians' to quit the Afro-Asian forum: 'it is her dispute with China that broke the back of Afro-Asia across the ridges of the Himalayas'.[1] But if this happened, what point would there be in Afro-Asian meetings? It is much more likely that the combination of embarrassment over the Sino-Indian dispute, and relief at the withdrawal of the tide of militancy, will keep Third World states away from declamatory conferences in the future.

If they confine themselves mainly to the UN, how will they combine there? The issues which arise will have much to do with the combinations that take place: the perennial Palestine issue has kept the Arab group in being, and the Congo affair and the struggle for Algeria brought to the surface divisions amongst African states which might otherwise have proved less prominent. The continuation of Portuguese colonialism and South African racial discrimination will encourage unity amongst African states to some extent; but if these settle into a stalemate they will decline as issues in their own right, and the African states may find little practical reason to combine, except where advantage is to be gained in procedural matters and in fields such as technical assistance. Some major change in events, such as a sudden spread of war in Southeast Asia, could certainly lead to a closing of ranks among some Afro-Asians. But it is more realistic to think of them as preserving the framework of their caucusing groups while showing, in practice, more interest in relations with the major powers than with one another.

Connexions with major powers

As we have seen, the major powers like to support declaratory resolutions from the Third World where these involve no sacrifice, but their main interest lies in the

[1] G. H. Jansen, *Afro-Asia and Non-Alignment* (1966), pp. 398-9.

special relations they can develop with particular Third World countries. The present circumstances of international life favour a considerable diversification of such relations. There is no longer the duopoly of two nuclear powers that seemed to polarize the world in the 1950s; China and France now try to create blocs or groups with loyalties to themselves, in competition with the USA and the Soviet Union. The fact that all four (and Britain) possess nuclear weapons gives some plausibility to equality of status between them, in spite of their disparity in striking power. This relative balance between a number of major powers has produced certain consequences. One is that, while Britain, France, and China have been released from their former direct dependence on the USA and the Soviet Union, smaller states of substance have not been so released. Thus states like Canada and Australia on the one side, and Czechoslovakia and Poland on the other, have hardly moved away from their earlier positions. This has repercussions in the Third World, in the sense that the international system has not achieved complete fluidity, but still contains 'camps' or 'sides' to which it may be important to belong. Thus, for a state such as Thailand, it may still be important to act as if the date were 1956, not 1966; and the possession by China of nuclear weapons may strengthen this view rather than alter it.

A second consequence acts in the opposite way. Although this multi-polar world is not completely fluid, it is still much more flexible than the world as seen from Bandung; and many, probably most, Third World states do not feel any urge towards permanent alignment, but are inclined to look about for opportunities to profit from the competing major powers' offers. India and the UAR are the most notable instances of countries which have managed to get help from more than one major power. At the same time, however, it is clear that the biggest aid-giving powers, the USA and the Soviet Union, are not prepared to go on raising their bids indefinitely. Each looks increasingly for value for money. The value need not be in undeviating support for American or Russian policies, but may be in terms of better opportunities in trade and investment, closer co-operation in military systems, or simply in the repayment of the money owed. Thus Third World countries are faced not only with opportunities to benefit from the flexibility of multi-polar situations, but also with obligations to behave themselves. The major powers may not be able to exercise heavy sanctions against countries which default in this way or that, but they may become mutually disenchanted. A Third World country may have to guard against a situation in which nobody wants to help it. There are, after all, plenty of others prepared to co-operate.

A third consequence of the relative balance is a freer international atmosphere, which allows for greater emphasis upon economic relations because of less emphasis upon security. It coincides with a situation in which anti-colonialism is less urgent, and more interest can be shown by Third World countries in special arrangements with European investors without incurring vituperation from international militants. The increasing influence in the Third World of West Germany, which is not a nuclear power and has hardly any ex-colonial links with Africa and Asia, but which has much to offer in technology and trade, shows what attractions a strictly economic approach can have.

These consequences of multi-polarity suggest that the major powers will continue to seek followers, from whom they may not be able to expect much more than a loose connexion and reasonable behaviour in paying debts. Any connexions are unlikely to be exclusive. Third World countries will be able to 'shop around', except where their existing arrangements are very tight, as with Thailand in security and the former French colonies in economy. How successful are the major powers likely to be in attracting their retinues?

The most interesting recent policy has been that of France. As we have seen, France has been more successful than Britain in keeping former African colonies in close association, because the French colonial system bound them closely to France in culture and economy, and they have had little alternative to pursue. But Gaullist ambitions go well beyond former French possessions in an attempt to marshal Third World opinion behind France. President de Gaulle has argued that there is a place for France to fill as leader of those countries which, while non-Communist, recognize that there is little danger of war between the Soviet Union and the Western powers, and wish to profit from the easier atmosphere which results. He has attempted to rally opinion in the Middle East and Latin America; and French spokesmen claim that the French position at UNCTAD was much closer to the Third World countries' demands than the American, the British, or the Russian. This French line is intriguing, but has little that is solid to offer Third World states. It gives them a talking-point if they are pressed heavily by the USA to support it; but France is not in most circumstances an alternative to the USA, and if a Third World state really needs American help it cannot escape the consequences by saying that the French see things differently. Moreover, it is widely recognized that, whatever the French may say about their interest in the Third World as a whole, they concentrate their substantial activities in their former colonies. It seems likely that only those ex-colonies will consistently support French initiatives, but that there will be some propaganda value for France in the Gaullist flourishes, and that French policy on continued colonialism (e.g. in New Caledonia) and on nuclear testing will get rather less obloquy than it would otherwise.

After a strenuous British effort in the 1950s to keep the Commonwealth of Nations as an area of broad British influence, the 1960s are witnessing an increasing disenchantment with its possibilities. Continued turmoil in Africa, together with British impatience about the influence of the sterling area and traditional Commonwealth trade in preventing an effective British bargain with the EEC, have combined to make the Commonwealth unpopular amongst many public men to whom it was formerly attractive. It is too soon to tell whether this unpopularity will lead to a wholesale abandonment of special concessions to Commonwealth members. It is fair to say, however, that Britain has little prospect of any special influence with Third World states except for those now in the Commonwealth: the Middle East is not an area in which Britain is popular, and Southeast Asia is dominated by other considerations. However, British economic influence in most African Commonwealth countries is indirect, and there is likely to be no British military guarantee to any Commonwealth country after confrontation ceases between Malaysia and Indonesia. In the circumstances, there is little that a British government anxious to make bargains with Western Europe can do to retain a special place in the affections of former colonies in Asia and Africa.

It is curious that the British should react so strongly against the Commonwealth because of the irritations produced by some of its argumentative Afro-Asian members. In the 1950s the principal argument used by British spokesmen for the Commonwealth was precisely that it brought together countries from a number of continents, aligned and non-aligned, white and coloured, new and old. Furthermore, it was sometimes claimed that British foreign policy gained room for manoeuvre through access to Asian countries, especially during Sir Anthony Eden's fencing with Mr Dulles over Quemoy and Matsu and over Vietnam. India was then regarded as a valuable auxiliary, and the Commonwealth as a means of enhancing British stature in the world. Conceivably, the African countries might be useful in a similar way. British impatience may stem in part from a disinclination to recognize the potential international importance of these countries, so recently colonial and so often preoccupied with colonial issues: it is significant that the African countries' reaction to Britain's last major colonial problem, the Rhodesia issue, has been responsible for more of this impatience and disenchantment than anything else. When that issue is finished, a natural sympathy between Britain and Commonwealth countries in Africa may reassert itself, provided there is no further friction over South Africa or South West Africa. But there will be no 'British group' in the Third World comparable with the French group; and the French group may suffer disintegration if political forces within France itself become impatient about paying the heavy bill for French aid.

The United States will presumably try to rally Third World opinion wherever its vital interests do not suffer. As the biggest aid-giver, it is subject to more pressure from the Third World than other major powers, and has, in addition, the responsibility for military and economic aid to Latin America. Having only one ingredient for a group in the shape of former colonies, it will presumably continue to concentrate upon a group of close allies, such as South Korea, Japan, and Thailand, as the foundation of its deterrence of China, and attempt beyond that to counter Russian and Chinese influence wherever these seem prominent in the Middle East and Africa. The Soviet Union may be expected to do the same in reverse, with special attention to areas near its borders, especially the Middle East and India. The clash of interests between the two super-powers can be seen in the UAR and India, where their influences meet directly and where local régimes are strong enough to keep them both in play. It is significant that, in spite of much Russian hubbub about Western plots in the Middle East, the Indians and Egyptians do not seem to have great difficulty in accommodating the Soviet Union and the USA as benevolent associates. None of the black African countries is sufficiently important to either the Russians or the Americans to warrant the same intense but effective competition as India and the UAR. In any case, Russian economic support of militant states such as Ghana and Mali was cautious, in spite of the propaganda claims made for it; and it seems unlikely that, with the general decline of Third World militancy, the Russians will see much advantage in trying to obtain client states in Africa. Experience in Indonesia, into which they put a great deal of money, only to see militancy overreach itself, may make them more cautious still. In my view, they will concentrate more in future upon propaganda than action, unless competition with the Chinese forces them into unwonted activity. China remains the enigma amongst the major powers; and in the final chapter I hope to suggest some alternative courses which it may follow.

In general, it would unwise to expect much more of solid connexions between major powers and Third World states than of connexions within the Third World itself.

Mending fences

If my analysis in this chapter is correct, we may find that two of the interests postulated for Third World states at the start prove the most important to the majority of them in the next decade: the improvement of the economy and the maintenance of good terms with neighbours. Both are interests closely connected with the domestic circumstances of most Third World states. Both involve enduring problems which, while they may sometimes be masked, do not disappear because of some striking action in another sphere. The fundamental difficulties of the Egyptian economy, for example, have persisted in spite of the wide-ranging character of President Nasser's foreign policy and the thoroughness of his domestic reforms. They call for foreign aid to harness new resources, and to augment the inadequate food supply provided by the present use of land. Increasingly, the demands of the economy seem to have limited the directions in which the UAR could move, although the volatile nature of the Middle East, and Egypt's central position there, still allow for some extra room. Necessarily, however, the wildest dreams of Arab unity have to be seen in the context of economic weakness. In a similar way, each small African government looks for ways in which production can be improved, the legacy of colonialism improved on, and the community rendered content. The lessons of Ghana and Indonesia, both of which squandered a rich heritage and had to begin again with requests for help in financing basic imports, will not be lost on poorer states in Africa and Asia. It is becoming more widely recognized that foreign aid, while desirable for economic improvement, will be neither big enough nor flexible enough to ensure economic growth. Each state has to work out its own combination of domestic planning and foreign assistance, whether through bilateral deals or the intervention of international bodies. If we assume a generally peaceful world, in which local conflicts do not become continental in character, Third World states may be expected to preoccupy themselves with their economies and to see a good many of their international connexions in the light of the help they can give to economic growth.

This will mean that West Germany and Japan, as industrial powers which are outside the nuclear prestige race but capable of a substantial impact on the economies of friendly states, will increase their international influence. The main point, however, is that economic demands will show themselves to be increasingly incapable of being satisfied by political connexions—i.e. that broad unity of view with a major power will not be sufficient to ensure the economic health of Third World states. They will seek wider connexions and more flexible opportunities, in much the same way as the states of Eastern Europe increasingly seek these outside the orbit of the Soviet Union.

On the political side, relations with neighbours will presumably be the main concern of most Third World states if, as I have suggested, Afro-Asianism declines as a consuming interest, and the nuclear balance allows most states not to align themselves with a single major power. In practice, difficulties with neighbours would probably bulk largest whatever happened; in some areas, of which the Middle East and Southern Africa are the most obvious, this is plainly so, and in others, notably South and South-east Asia, the certainty of clashes between neighbours is to some extent obscured by the intervention of major powers from outside. It may become increasingly difficult to discern a Third World at all, or even an Asia or an Africa, except on those ceremonial occasions which constitute the minimum level of engagement in Afro-Asian affairs.

The fact that continental and all-embracing activities become less obligatory, and local matters more pressing, need not prevent a sudden revival of Afro-Asian fervour if there is a significant shift in world conditions. It is possible that, if one or more of the basic elements of the world situation changes, some Afro-Asian countries might try to regain some form of unity to meet the new situation. Such major changes are discussed in the final chapter.

5

Vulgar Errors

In this short, dogmatic chapter I attack certain illusions about the Third World. They are often heard in conversation and read in editorials. They are not supposed to form part of intelligent argument, but they occur more often in academic discussions than most academics would be prepared to admit.

Harmony and disharmony

The very notion of a 'Third World' induces the idea of harmony amongst the members, and suggests, if not a bloc or front, at least a force of some kind. Sometimes it is good, sometimes bad. Vaguely leftist opinion often assumes that Asians and Africans are united in disapproval of everything the West does: *these are revolutionary states which are marching towards a better future*. Vague rightists put it differently: *the Afro-Asians are gunning for the rest of us*, even *they want to make us poor like themselves*. But there are also those who see nothing but dismarmony amongst the states of the Third World. *They really hate each other, you know* is sometimes heard from people with experience of the communal disputes of many countries in Africa and Asia.

The truth is somewhere in between. The preceding chapters should have shown that there is no obvious harmony of interests between Afro-Asian states, whatever is said by them in propaganda. At the extreme of disharmony, there are the bitter disputes between certain Arab states, the arguments over boundaries (between Algeria and Morocco, Ghana and Togo, Kenya and Somalia, India and Pakistan, and, sometimes, as with Morocco's attitude to Mauritania, a denial of a state's very right to exist), the struggles over communalism (as between Malaya and Singapore) and the deliberate policies which incite war, as with Indonesia's confrontation of Malaysia. In economic terms, in spite of the common demands of Third World states for special treatment by the developed countries, there are all the elements of competition and jealousy: states with comparable exports abuse others which have obtained special concessions, as when the francophone states of West Africa were given associate status by the EEC; states in a potential federation, such as Kenya, Uganda, and Tanzania, cannot agree on its terms because one might get more out of it than others; South-east Asian states, invited to enter into long-term economic arrangements with Japan and India, are reluctant to do so because of their fear of being overwhelmed. Joint ventures are difficult to organize, mutual benefit does not often survive the speeches in which it is postulated. India and Pakistan might serve as giant exemplars of the difficulties which seem to be inherent in any attempt to pose harmony as a natural condition amongst Afro-Asian states. To the outsider, few states have so much to gain from co-operation: they divide a sub-continent, they have a common administrative heritage, they are engaged in wasteful competition in spheres where they used to be integrated, they can enjoy joint use of certain natural resources which will otherwise go to waste. Yet, for nearly twenty years, they have lived in a state of armed truce tempered by the occasional foray. Harmony is so easy to advocate because of the obvious benefits that would flow from it; disharmony is so obviously the actual state of things.

But we should not fly to the other extreme and assert

that Afro-Asian states can never co-operate and are doomed to perpetual conflict. In certain ways they do co-operate. There was considerable discipline at UNCTAD. Afro-Asian coalitions at the UN often thrash out amongst themselves agreed compromises which serve the causes they are attempting to forward. There is a modified degree of technical assistance between neighbouring countries in Asia and Africa, and it is frequent to find arguments of much subtlety, issuing from consultation between interested Third World states, at international conferences. But it is only on the major, all-embracing issues of colonialism, racial discrimination, and economic development that the Afro-Asian states can all be brought into the same team, to work together for declaratory resolutions and to urge international action. It is not surprising that this should be so; it would be surprising if overall co-operation between them went any further. They have, in fact, much the same capacity for co-operation as any other group of diverse states in history. They can be summoned for a time to particular standards, but their support of those standards will depend, in the long run, upon the estimate each makes of the effect upon itself. In the 1950s and 1960s, resistance to colonialism and racial discrimination has been easy, since so much of it has rested upon declaratory statements which involve no sacrifice. Efforts to boycott or invade the recalcitrant régimes have been grandiose in planning but insignificant in operation. The great causes prove to have little force when it is necessary to take risks in support of them. The interdependence of economies may often be such that no country can afford to go on for long denying itself the products of another, in spite of the latter's bad behaviour; even the Chinese, it is said, import mealies from South Africa.

The Third World countries are not out to despoil the developed countries, but they consider that a debt is owed to them because of their part in the previous economic development of those others. The issue is highly debatable, but there is much to be said on the Third World side. It is neither surprising nor immoral for the poor to consider that the rich have a duty towards them. The whole notion of despoilation, so often voiced by fanatics in Western countries, is misplaced. What the Third World asks for, in the rare moments when it speaks with one voice, is the means to buy things from the richer countries; both sides can only be enriched by the development of resources which are waiting to be tapped. While much play is made with questions of population and starvation, the basis of the Third World demands is investment which will bring returns on both sides; it is not a bread-line operation, except in those extreme cases where starvation has set in.

Beyond the issues of colonialism and racial discrimination, only economic development can create overall harmony amongst Afro-Asians, and then only for declaratory purposes. There will be no general war because Negroes are ill-treated in either South Africa or Alabama. Established states in the Third World have too much to lose.

Leadership

A good deal of nonsense is talked about leadership amongst the Third World countries. In fact, there is very little. It is sometimes said that *India and China are the models which Afro-Asian countries must adopt;* or that *Nasser is trying to get Africa as well as the Middle East in his grip;* or that, in the long run, *the Russians (or the Chinese) must take over.* Contrary to much of what is written, Afro-Asian countries do not normally look for leadership at all. When very new to the international scene, they may look for guidance over procedure and sometimes broad policy to established states; when seeking particular forms of technical operation, whether in the economy or in government, they will look around for models; when trying to cut a figure at international conferences and the UN, they will look for causes which seem congenial. But none of these involves seeking a leader in the sense of looking for a country to guide them permanently, or to give them a model on which their whole social system is to be based. They are, in fact, highly eclectic in their choice of models in minor matters. In spite of much hubbub from the Arabs and the Chinese, experts from Israel and Taiwan are to be found in a number of African states. The main point is that states which are conscious of their inability to do all that needs to be done for themselves will look for help where they can get it, and will not be inhibited by the implications of the resolutions at conferences, unless those resolutions are backed by unpleasant consequences for disobedience. But each state's government sees itself as sufficient in its conception of a social system, of economic progress, and of foreign policy; however much is borrowed, what is done is quickly thought to be local, indeed autochthonous.

It is true that states do aspire to leadership in the Third World. At various times India, Egypt, and Ghana have tried to play this part. But the situations in which they were able to give a credible performance were temporary, not permanent. India, as the first and biggest newly independent country after World War II, had the sort of natural role in leadership which was seen at Delhi in 1947, and, to a lesser extent, at Bandung in 1955: a role compounded of diplomatic expertise, enunciation of broad, acceptable principles, and assertion of the need for dignity and esteem for the new states But difficulties arose when India wanted its own national interests, as over Kashmir, accepted by other states in spite of the problems that this might cause them. And India's clash with China created a quarrel into which other Third World states did not want to enter. Egypt's symbolic position was prominent and widely accepted after its invasion by British, French, and Israeli troops in 1956, and its international aims have earned wide acceptance. But, again, its attempt to impose its own interests upon others have frequently led to opposition, in the Arab group and outside it. There is, moreover, little disposition amongst black African states to accept guidance from Asian and Middle Eastern states, which are remote and which, in some cases, raise the delicate matter of Muslim unity for countries which are not primarily Muslim in composition. Ghana's chances of leadership in Africa arose from its being first of the new African states. In early pan-African arrangements, due deference was paid to this fact. But the increasing militancy and personalism of President Nkrumah's policy alienated many potential supporters, and his tendency to harbour rebels from neighbouring states made him suspect as a trouble-maker. By 1966 the initial advantage had been lost.

The assertion that the Russians or the Chinese will win in the end is best left for separate treatment, but it is enough to say here that no African or Asian government believes in a basic determinism at work in favour of the major Communist powers, unless it be those which are small and located close to the borders of China. Even there, the sense of independence is strong. As we have seen, both Russians and Chinese possess advantages over the Western countries in certain ways, but they have disadvantages too; and, as major powers, they are just as liable to charges of 'great-power chauvinism'. The pressures which Russians and Chinese have tried to put on Afro-Asian states in their clashes with one another over representation at this and that meeting have deeply offended many of those whom they have tried to persuade. This sort of offence may be only skin-deep in diplomats and ministers who wish to be regarded as somebodies and not as puppets, but it helps to build up attitudes which may be important in foreign policy. Neither Russia nor China has inducements strong enough to persuade any state voluntarily to exchange its present régime for the kind of acquiescent body which those powers want; even the Congo (Brazzaville) has proved recalcitrant.

Communism

The main difficulty in regard to Communism and the Third World is the rooted determinism of many Western thinkers. The special form of this determinism is the belief that *these states will go Communist because they are poor*. With varying degrees of sophistication, writers and speakers postulate an unavoidable choice between Communism and such vastly improved economic conditions as few Third World states can hope to see. But this is all assumption. No state has gone Communist simply because it was poor. The Soviet Union became Communist because of war-weariness and the seizure of power at a decisive moment by a minority which governed through force; the East European states became Communist because of Soviet military occupation, as did North Korea; China became Communist in circumstances not dissimilar to those of the Soviet Union, but with a difference in scale; North Vietnam has become Communist under the stress of war, and Cuba, if it is Communist, under the threat of it. War is the constant theme, not poverty, although no one would assert that war was a sole requirement for Communism. The Soviet Union and the East European states were not noticeably amongst the poorest countries before they got Communist governments, although they were wasted by war. China and North Vietnam are really the nearest we can get to examples, and in both cases war is the decisive element, not poverty, though neither was an advanced state.

Western determinism in this matter arises from an extension of economic determinism, the belief that economic conditions decide all other conditions. But there is no case so far for thinking this is so. Communist revolts have been defeated in Indonesia, Malaya, Burma, the Philippines, and India. Although there was Western help in some cases, there is no evidence that the Communists had anything like majority support. In Africa no Communist party is legal, and few exist under cover. Parties would be hard to organize in the countries where they are prohibited, even if the bans were removed. No doubt the Soviet Union and China would gladly take the chances which war offered to impose Communist régimes in countries over which they could exercise some control, as in Eastern Europe and North Korea. The Chinese emphasis upon armed revolt in the colonial areas can be interpreted in this way. The Russians' emphasis upon peaceful coexistence would seem to apply with force only at the highest international level: they were not noticeably disturbed by the Vietnam conflict until the United States took a prominent part in it. But this Chinese and Russian eagerness is no reason why we should regard communization of Third World states as a foregone conclusion. Armed effort on any scale by either power would probably be opposed by the United States. The force of Afro-Asian opinion, whether muted or outspoken, would be brought to bear against them if they seemed to be causing wars for their own purposes.

There is another recurrent illusion which bears rather less examination: that *these are really Communist states in disguise*. At various times Sukarno, Nasser, Nkrumah, and even Nehru have been styled Communists. The fault here is in not distinguishing between Communist régimes and those which at times receive Communist support because they are carrying out policies, or voicing opinions, of which the Communist states approve. There is no reason to believe that any of the leaders in question were Communists, whether they flirted with Communist parties in their youth or not. The point about each of their régimes is that it was stridently nationalist, with strong overtones of denunciation of this or that Western policy; it was the latter which the Communists applauded. They deplored the former.

The basic point is that the questions of anti-colonialism and racial discrimination have given the Communist powers advantages, since they can claim that these are practices which they do not indulge in. But neither do all the Western states. There is no necessary relation between non-Communism and colonialism; in fact, it could be argued that it is the least typical Western states which will be the last colonialists: Portugal and Spain.

The Communist states do get some special advantage in the Third World, from the attraction of their economic systems on paper. But it is one thing for a future finance minister to pore over Communist pamphlets when he is a needy student in a colonialist environment, and another for him to wish to adopt Communist policies when he has come to office. The drawbacks of the Communist system quickly become apparent, especially in agriculture; the disparity in resources between his own country and China or the Soviet Union is clear; the special wishes, aims, customs, and values of his own people, to whom as a nationalist he is attached, make themselves felt. The advent of practicality will not make him refuse to accept aid from Communist countries, but it will make him cautious of total Communist prescriptions. There has been a remarkably uniform reaction of this kind from Third World countries.

There is no saying how far Communist power might spread if major war broke out. But there is no necessary connexion between the poverty of new states and any disposition to embrace Communism as a native faith. Western talkers often assume that there is, either because they have surrendered to unproved determinism in this matter, or because they equate disagreement with Western interests and Communist leanings. The two are not the same, however much the Communist states might try to make them appear so.

Western connexions

As one might expect, there is a whole forest of Western clichés and illusions about the states of the Third World. *They hate us*, says one group. *They really want us back, if it wasn't for the demagogues*, says another. *They're incapable of moving into the modern world*, it is sometimes alleged. *Things would be all right if it wasn't for the memory of colonialism*, Americans are tempted to say. In reply it is often suggested that *we really know these people; it is the Americans who are messing things up by interfering.*

In most Third World countries there are forces which tend towards connexion with the West and forces which press in the opposite direction. People with a background of Western ways and Western experience will often be in the first group; so will those who have business interests which they think will be better served by Western links. On the other side will be those who identify the West with the colonialist tradition and who think that their country was mulcted by the West for its own advantage. Those in revolt against the local social system, with its traditionalist elements, will often blame the West for nourishing these elements instead of introducing more modern and progressive institutions. The cleavage between these two groups may often be wide. But it is frequently over-emphasized by Western observers and commentators, who seize upon the extreme statements by either side and assume a social gulf as wide and permanent as these statements on paper would suggest. In fact, however, many of those on the latter side, who attack the West in the abstract, are attracted by its ways and opportunities, and are often in opposition to it, not because it is inherently evil, but because they cannot command the expectations which are common in Western countries. If one looks at the matter in detail, it is clear that most Third World countries value and try to enhance their links with the West. This is certainly true of nearly all the francophone states; it is true of each of the Commonwealth states, whatever wounding things may have been said in the heat of debate; it is true of traditionalist régimes like those of Iran and Ethiopia, which are still glad to get Western investment and training; it is even true of an Arab state such as Egypt, with good reason to dislike Western countries and with close economic connexions with the Soviet bloc.

The main Western complaints, however, are not about these vital but humdrum connexions, but about the refusal of Third World states at crucial times to follow Western policy. The two great areas of divergence have been colonialism and military pacts. The latter is dealt with below. The colonialism issue is one on which it must be accepted that Third World states will refuse to take all Western statements at face value, because their leaders have often found those statements to be false in their own cases, and because anti-colonialism is, of necessity, a binding force within and between Afro-Asian states, to an extent which no government can ignore. No matter how ritualistic anti-colonial observance may become, it is still a matter of continuing concern. Yet only the blindest of Western observers can contend that the Third World states have been either uniform or unfeeling in their approach to colonial questions. Only Western intransigence has provoked their united condemnation. Where colonial powers have shown themselves prepared to talk and act in ways which showed their sincerity in wishing to emancipate their coloured subjects, the clamour has been small. An example can be seen in Australian New Guinea. Consistently, the Soviet Union has tried to provoke Third World states into unconditional censure of Australian administration; yet it has not succeeded, and UN missions to the Trust Territory have usually been understanding and moderate in their demands. Few Third World states owe Australia debts of gratitude. If the anti-colonialist crusade had been unreasoning and unscrupulous Australia would have made a prime object of scorn. In fact, the difficulties of the problem have been generally recognized.

It is useless to expect former colonial territories to want their masters back. Their whole frame of reference changes when they become independent, in spite of the prevalence of institutions founded under colonial rule. There is no going back on this path. Nor is there any reason to believe that significant numbers of people want it retraced, except some of those whose livelihoods depended directly on the patronage of the colonial power. New interests quickly become established in every post-colonial society. New horizons appear when independence comes; many cannot be reached, but some can, and they usually prove sufficient in themselves. As we have seen, help is welcomed from most quarters, including the former rulers, provided they behave themselves; but one feat of local management, such as Egypt's proven ability to operate the Suez Canal successfully on its own, is valued more highly than any help from outside. Whether the British or French or Americans are most welcome, and most successful, is a matter of judgement by the state in question. Small states in Southeast Asia such as Cambodia and Singapore may find the former colonial power a better friend than the United States; Prince Sihanouk and Mr Lee Kuan Yew have, at any rate, expressed themselves in something like these terms. But they do not wish to prostrate themselves before anyone, and they will no doubt accept American assistance if the conditions for it improve.

The West cannot expect the Third World to fawn on it, but it need not expect universal denigration. New states in a condition of excited nationalism are always hard to live with, wherever they arise; Africa and Asia are no exception. But the use of judgement and good sense by Western states, along with a full awareness of the dignity felt by any country, however small, that attains the status of a sovereign state, brings dividends in all sorts of ways. It is only if expectations are set unreasonably high that the illusions mentioned above gain plausibility.

Non-alignment

Two contrary illusions are current about the Third World states and non-alignment: *non-alignment is their natural posture*, and *non-alignment is a Communist trick*. The second has already been touched on in Chapter 5. Non-alignment was not a Communist invention; at first it was viewed by the Soviet Union with disfavour, as an attempt to blind the peoples of Asian countries to their obligation to support the progressive side. Later, when it became clear that the non-aligned position of a state like India might work in ways which suited Soviet interests, non-alignment became more respectable in Communist eyes, although states were condemned for departing from it only when they leaned towards the Western point of view. Undoubtedly, Western policy might have gone more smoothly and successfully if non-alignment had not been put forward. But, as we saw in Chapter 5, the difficulties of the 1950s were surmounted, not by the West's success or failure in settling up SEATO's and CENTO's, but by the growth of a nuclear stalemate; non-alignment is now a policy which can be talked about but need not be pursued with the intensity of the 1950s. It is now a turn of phrase, rather than a vital interest.

The view that non-alignment is a natural posture for Afro-Asian states is widely held in Western circles, especially amongst intellectuals; it is also propagated at various times by Third World states such as Egypt, India, and Algeria. There is much plausibility in the view, since it is clear that no Third World state wants alignment for its own sake, and each would prefer to keep out of the quarrels of the major powers if it can. Put in a form which applies to states which are in no danger from major powers nearby, and which can see some guarantee of forebearance by the other major powers if they keep themselves to themselves, it is, to a large extent, natural: it is a kind of policy of repose analogous to that of the human body, which remains at rest when it has no reason to be moving in a particular direction. But the difficulty arises with states which do see a threat from a major power, and wish to insure against it. If the idea of non-alignment as 'natural' is extended to situations in which a government wishes to insure itself, in an attempt to force the government into refusing the insurance, this is interference with sovereignty as great as any which insists, from the opposite side, that a state must be aligned. At various times Thailand, the Philippines, Iraq, Turkey, Pakistan, and other states have felt the need of insurance. Even India, once it found China wanting, entered into something like alignment with the Soviet Union and the United States against China.

The position of most Third World states is quite simple:

they wish to defend themselves by whatever means seem appropriate, whether collective or individual, but they do not wish to enter into quarrels which they do not feel are theirs. Two recent cases of attempts to align them will indicate how predominant opinion runs. At the tenth anniversary celebrations of the Bandung Conference in Djakarta in April 1965, it seemed to a number of the African and Asian delegates that President Sukarno was asking them to give up non-alignment in favour of alignment with China in whatever struggle might appeal to China and Indonesia. The President's announcement that there would be a CONEFO (Conference of the New Emergent Forces) in 1966 made many of them think that this body would be a Sino-Indonesian substitute for the UN, from which Indonesia had resigned; and they were markedly cool to the idea that they should simultaneously desert the UN and range themselves alongside régimes which were regarded as adversaries of Western powers. President Sukarno's attempt at a forced alignment was a failure.

The nearest approach which the United States now makes to a 'stand up and be counted' demand upon Third World states is its annual attempt to keep the Communist Chinese out of the China seat in the UN. This is not an instance of military alignment, but Third World states are being asked to assent to a body of doctrine about China which is widely regarded as particularly American. It is noticeable that most African states do not wish to commit themselves. They may have views about the place of China in world politics, but they do not want to be counted on one side or the other in a matter which seems to many of them ritualistic and to others a survival from quarrels at other times and places. The American government has become more aware of this sentiment and less anxious to press the point.

It is likely that non-alignment will survive in something like the same way as monarchy survives in Britain: as a frequently useful but not essential aspect of policy, which would be difficult to dispose of but is not permitted to stand in the way of necessary action when a government is convinced that action must be taken.

Nationalism

Nationalism in Asia and Africa, but especially in Africa, often comes under heavy fire in Western conversation and even in the lecture room. *The boundaries are totally artificial*, it is pointed out. *You need something distinctive to found nationalism on.* Furthermore, it is felt that only large units can survive: *it's absurd to think of these little places as nation-states.* In any case, *nationalism is a Western thing.* It is sometimes said that *nationalism is just a cover for neo-colonialism (or Communism).*

Some of these statements stem from semantic difficulties about the basis of nationalism. If one assumes that a distinctive social attribute such as a common language or religion, or a distinctive country with prominent natural boundaries, is essential to the existence of nationalism, many of the states of the Third World have no claim to the term. Similarly, if the whole emphasis is laid on homogeneity of the community, states with a mixture of peoples can hardly be called national. My own view is that any government can display nationalism, in the sense of attachment to the country and its people, attempts to advance their welfare, and determination to prevent others from interfering with it. When a government acts along these lines, it seems to me to be pursuing a national policy; if the action is extreme, one may call it nationalistic. The real difference lies between those who insist that nationalism, to be legitimate, must stem from the people themselves and be felt as a natural emanation, and those who believe that a concerted feeling can be nourished from above by the deliberate exercise of state policy. The latter seems to me the more satisfactory, since it allows us to give the main emphasis to the actions of governments; and, as we saw in Chapter 1, the nationalism characteristic of new Afro-Asian states is essentially positive state nationalism, with its deliberate attempt to unite the people around the symbols and achievements of the government. If I am right, then much of the criticism in the statements above falls to the ground. Boundaries need not matter; size can be unimportant; the absence of local traditions may be an advantage—provided the government makes strong and successful efforts to instil discipline and unity. It is in the nature of states to try to make their peoples more loyal by making them ever more dependent upon the state for safety and comfort. Third World states strive to maximize their peoples' living standards, and in the process to weld them into units which will accept the government's will. To a considerable extent, this policy is successful. It cannot be entirely so, since natural pluralism continually struggles against efforts at uniformity: not all interests can be accommodated within the one set of policies. But a good deal can be done in most cases, with the help of army and police.

The view that nationalism is a Western thing, and therefore cannot be found in its true form outside areas of European culture and settlement, rests upon defining nationalism in ways which stress Europe's experience. It would be better to recognize that the formal expression of nationalism in Europe, the sovereign state, is Europe's most significant export to other continents: long before it was a significant factor in Africa it had shown its vitality in Latin America, amongst people for whom boundaries were often as casual and unrelated to either culture or geography, as they were later to be in Africa. The sovereign state moulds its people through the instruments which it puts in the hands of governments: the tools of taxation, military service, border control, tariff protection, separate school systems, local political symbols, police power, and the like. Asian and African governments, whatever the pasts of their countries, have been adept at using these, to evoke patriotism and the general view that one's first loyalty lies towards one's country as exemplified by its government.

It is possible, of course, that those who stress the inadequacy of many boundaries and the unviability of particular states may be proved right in the long run, by a gradual amalgamation of state units and the creation of larger states with viable economies. But the whole trend since World War II, except in certain trading areas, has been in the other direction, towards the splitting up of federations and the assertion of local autonomy. It would be unwise to regard this trend as freakish. There is no more determinism about small countries seeking to melt into large ones than in poor countries seeking to become Communist.

It is safest, in fact, to expect a strong-minded nationalism from *any* state, however small and lacking in a unified past.

Power

Two over-simplified statements are often heard about the Third World states in relation to power: *they have rejected power;* and *they only understand naked power.*

Power, like nationalism, is a word which invites semantic argument. If we take it to mean coercion by one state over another (or one over a group, or one group over another), we have a manageable definition. The coercion may take various forms, but armed force and economic deprivation are the most obvious. In this sense, there is plenty of power in the Third World. Indonesian confronttation of Malaysia, Arab raids on Israel, border clashes between Algeria and Morocco, Egyptian intervention in the Yemen, are all cases of power in the service of national policy. Moreover, it is characteristic of many Third World states that naked power is never far removed from their internal situations. Many depend upon the army and police to put down disorder and revolt. Many have shown —as in the Congo, Indonesia, and in the partition of India —that the use of arms against one's local enemies is acceptable to their peoples. It is thus wrong in almost every sense to say that Third World states have 'rejected' power. They use it when they think it appropriate.

It might be argued, however, that they had rejected power politics, in the sense that they disapproved of the coercion of one state by others. This might be so in the abstract. But it is untrue of the Arab states of the Middle East in regard to Israel, or of most African states in regard to Portugal and South Africa. The coercion of these states is welcomed. The argument is that they have done things which put them outside the pale of protection of sovereignty, and that they should be punished. But these statements are the ordinary currency of international relations when the use of power is being justified; there is nothing to choose between their use by Third World states and by others. What might be said with some justice is that Third World states wish to insulate themselves from the quarrels of the major powers. But this has been true of small states from time immemorial; it has also been true that such states often seek protection against neighbours or major powers when the alternative is isolation, and this is the case with many states of the Third World now.

It is possible that some Third World states might disarm and forget the notion of power if the major powers did not use force against one another. But it is still characteristic of the world that major powers use force or the threat of it in their duels, although they usually do it at one remove, rather than directly. Suez and Vietnam are examples of how major powers use force in order, as they hope, to even the balance between themselves. But, as already suggested, they no longer use it directly against Third World countries, and they are becoming ever more subtle in the threat of it against one another: the nuclear balance calls for continual refinement in the degree of threat that can be used. They do not use naked power against Third World states; and this is not only because they fear the impact upon other major powers, but also because they recognize how clumsy a weapon naked power would be. It is not a question of the Afro-Asian countries 'understanding' naked power; every country understands the equivalent of a knife at its throat, if things come to such an extreme. It is rather that the effects of the nuclear balance, together with the multiplicity of Third World countries and of the differing interests to which their existence gives rise, call for more subtle and less dangerous methods. Whether this state of affairs can continue is the subject of the next chapter.

6

A Difficult Future

THE picture in Chapter 4 of a likely Afro-Asian future was of national interests dominating the actions of most states, of Afro-Asianism being maintained but very much at a discount, and of each state concerning itself with its immediate surroundings and its economic development. This seems the most likely future as things stand in mid-1966. But there are at least three areas of potential change in world affairs which might provide alterations to the picture. These are the areas of nuclear balance, Sino-Soviet relations, and world economics. Developments in certain others might be envisaged: for example, American withdrawal to a Fortress America, or a complete solidarity of interests between the USA and the Soviet Union. But such developments would not represent impulses of change in themselves so much as results following alterations in either nuclear balance or Sino-Soviet relations. The three named areas are those in which there is the greatest uncertainty.

Nuclear balance

The present nuclear balance has produced the relatively easy international atmosphere described in Chapter 4, and has given Third World states opportunities which they might not otherwise have had. It could be altered in two main ways. There could be a change of policy on the part of existing nuclear powers, and there could be a further proliferation of nuclear powers.

The existing nuclear powers do not use their weapons and do not pass them on to their allies, unless those allies are nuclear powers in their own right. In the case of the two super-powers, the USA and the Soviet Union, nuclear weapons are used for mutual deterrence: each knows that the other is equipped to do it great damage, and that nuclear warfare between them would be mutually unrewarding. It is recognized that nuclear attacks on a super-power's allies might be answered by nuclear retaliation by the other super-power; there is no certainty about this, but the risk involved is too great for either to contemplate in the circumstances so far experienced. The allies have not, however, been given nuclear weapons to use in their own right. The fact that Britain and France, which are allies of the USA, have developed their own weapons is not presumably regarded by either the USA or the Soviet Union as altering the fundamental balance between themselves, since it is most unlikely that either Britain or France would use these weapons unless in concert with the USA. French independence in general foreign policy is a reality under President de Gaulle, but it is not expected to produce a French initiative in nuclear war. British independence has never been viewed as likely to produce such an initiative. Thus, there is a basic equality of circumstance between the USA and the Soviet Union, which produces the fundamental nuclear balance. That balance is complicated for purposes of discussion by Britain and France, but far more complicated by the possession of nuclear weapons by China. Whereas the behaviour of France and Britain in regard to the super-powers is relatively predictable, that of China is much less so.

Both the USA and the Soviet Union can be regarded as in a state of nascent deterrence of China by their superiority in nuclear technology and in production of vehicles to deliver a nuclear bomb. China is as yet unable to inflict disaster on the major cities of the two other nuclear powers to which, in different ways, it is opposed; they are able to inflict such disaster on China's. China will presumably continue to develop in both areas of technology. But, even if it gets to a stage comparable with that now reached by the Soviet Union, it will still be unable to venture on a strike without risking disaster. Provided there is no return by the Soviet Union and China to the cordiality of the early 1950s, China will be unable to challenge either the Soviet Union or the USA in the field of their domestic security; if there is a rapprochement with the Soviet Union, China would still be unable to risk a blow at the USA without Russian approval, and would, in any case, probably not wish to take the risk, since China would then be within the area of Russian protection of which Eastern Europe is now the main part.

The maintenance of present policies and positions by the existing nuclear powers would, then, produce a continuing balance something like the present one. It is unlikely that the Western powers would change their present policy of not using nuclear weapons unless they were attacked by nuclear means; it is unlikely that the Soviet Union would try to attack them. Any problem which might affect the Third World arises from whether China would use nuclear weapons in an attempt to expand its power in Asia. Such a possibility can be viewed in two ways. Either China would deliberately use nuclear weapons in a war which it had started or in which it became engaged; or its generally threatening attitude would induce other countries to develop their own stock. In both cases, the Sino-Indian conflict is clearly the most likely source of trouble. India and China have already clashed, and quite possibly will do so again. We do not have enough knowledge of the inner processes of Chinese policy-making to guess whether the Chinese would deliberately contemplate the use of nuclear force against India; we can certainly imagine that India might develop nuclear weapons as a means of deterring China or of overcoming the natural advantages which the Chinese possess in hostilities along the northern borders of India.

Within the spectrum of the major powers, this departure from existing practice by China seems the most likely change. If we assume a generally greater recklessness on the part of China, corresponding in the use of nuclear weapons with its use in international discourse, then China might go even further, and equip its allies, North Vietnam and North Korea, with nuclear weapons, and so complicate the issue further. But China has shown more caution in deed than in word. India seems to be the opponent who might incite its use of nuclear weapons; the possibilities of the Sino-Indian situation, for the Third World and for the major powers, receive further consideration below.

Further nuclear proliferation could come from the existing nuclear powers' equipping others, or from the independent development of nuclear capacity by others. There is little likelihood of the first so far as all powers but China are concerned. The main possibility, as discussed by those who take up the issue of proliferation, is of the USA handing control of bombs to Western Germany. This would risk the destruction of the existing fragile confidence between the Soviet Union and the USA, and in this sense would make the whole world more unstable; but its direct impact on Third World states would be slight, and it might not affect them greatly even if West Germany became in independent nuclear power, since it might settle into the same position as Britain and France now occupy. But if China showed that it favoured nuclear dissemination amongst its close associates, this might well stimulate other countries to ask the United States for bombs or to develop their own. Japan and Australia are the most likely. Other Asian countries would then probably seek protection from either China or the United States, unless they were prepared to undertake the isolated and withdrawn role that Burma now fills. Any Chinese extension of nuclear power would thus be matched by an extension amongst some of the allies of the USA, presumably by an even stricter nuclear watch on China by the USA than is exercised now, and by a forced alignment of Asian states which might finally destroy the assumptions which linger from Bandung. Africa and the Middle East could be exempt from this forced alignment, and might see efforts to establish 'areas of peace' there, similar to Mr Nehru's earlier efforts. It is more likely, however, that African states would avert their faces from what was happening in Asia, in the hope that it would not come their way.

There are three Afro-Asian countries which might develop their own independent nuclear capacity in the next few years: Japan, India, and Egypt. Each is capable of doing so. Japan, the most capable but least likely, would probably cause the least stir. But if India and Egypt went nuclear, with their eyes on China and Pakistan in the one case, and Israel in the other, the potential disturbance would be great. Indeed, short of another eye-ball to eye-ball confrontation between two nuclear powers, as in Cuba in 1962, these two prospects are the most frightening of immediate nuclear possibilities. The fear would be, not so much of their immediate consequences, as of their capacity for chain reaction.

Of the two, the case of Egypt (and, equally, of Israel, since it may be assumed that any nuclear effort on the part of one would stimulate a similar effort by the other) is probably the more manageable, in the sense that it might prove more localized. China is insulated from the Middle East, and would not be able to affect the situation markedly. The United States and the Soviet Union would be anxious to keep the fire from spreading. They could be expected to offer great inducements to both Israel and Egypt not to develop nuclear weapons, and to warn these states' neighbours against interference if it came to a clash. Given the curious condition between peace and open war in which Egypt and Israel have been since 1956, it is possible that both might acquire primitive nuclear weapons and remain in the state of mutual deterrence in which the Soviet Union and the USA now stand at a more advanced level. If this deterrence failed, in the sense that war broke out with conventional weapons and one contestant used nuclear weapons in a last desperate throw, it is still possible that the conflict would not spread. The desire and capacity of the two super-powers to prevent its doing so would be considerable. But, even then, it might have dire ultimate consequences in convincing other potential users of nuclear weapons that their use did not mean general conflict, and so might be safely embarked upon. Any nuclear conflict between Israel and Egypt would undoubtedly cause a great furore amongst Afro-Asian states, but it would not necessarily alter their previous lines of policy, provided the super-powers managed to contain it.

The Sino-Indian position is much less manageable. Neither country is amenable to control in anything like the same way as Israel and Egypt in a crisis: sheer physical size is one reason, greater international stature another. As things stand, the matter of proliferation rests with India, which possesses the capacity to develop nuclear weapons but which so far, in spite of some internal promptings, has failed to do so. The decision has been based partly on economic grounds, partly on a strong desire to limit the area of nuclear danger. At the same time, Indian spokesmen have been critical of the philosophy of nonproliferation adopted by some of the nuclear powers, the practical outcome of which, in existing circumstances, would be that China could develop nuclear capacity and India would be denied it. If India and China became involved in another war which India lost, even though the Chinese did not use nuclear weapons, the internal pressure for India to go nuclear in order to avoid a later defeat would be very great. If China used nuclear weapons against an India which had deliberately decided not to equip itself with them, Indian leaders might be regarded by the historians of the future as having been recreant to their trust. There are thus good arguments for India's developing nuclear weapons—much better, indeed, than any that have ever been suggested for the French and British action in doing so. The arguments against this are obvious, especially the economic arguments. But when faced with the question of national survival they might not look compelling.

It would not be surprising if India decided that the risk of nuclear arms was worth taking. If it decided otherwise, it would be entitled to suggest to the United States and the Soviet Union that they support it both economically and militarily. How far they would go in the second of these directions would depend very much upon the state of trust between them, the degree of enmity which had been reached between the Soviet Union and China, and the assessment of their own interests which they had attached to India. It is difficult to believe that either, under present circumstances, would use nuclear weapons against a conventional Chinese attack on India. A nuclear attack might be another matter; but even here they would presumably come to India's aid with nuclear weapons only if they classed an attack on India as equivalent to an attack on themselves. How likely is this? Present indications do not provide sufficient evidence to enable us to say, any more than they enable us to decide whether the Chinese would risk either a conventional or nuclear attack. Much would presumably depend on whether the USA and the Soviet Union were preoccupied elsewhere.

This condition of general indecision, together with the explosive situation between India and China, and the attendant difficulties between India and Pakistan, make India's acquisition of nuclear weapons an open question. They also make the extent of Russian or American help to India an open question. Both could be resolved by pacific policies on the part of China. But, however unlikely these are from the present Chinese leadership, they become even less likely when one considers how much advantage China gains from the present uncertainty: indecisiveness on India's part; a steady lessening of Indian influence amongst other Afro-Asian countries; a general reluctance on the part of European powers to help stabilize the situation in Asia; the virtual isolation of the United States as a power determined to confront China; the support for China, or the neutral posture, of smaller Asian states frightened of eventual Chinese domination. The fact that India might be provoked into acquiring nuclear weapons may seem a small price for China to pay.

If both China and India possessed nuclear weapons, or if the confrontation between the United States and China grew perceptibly more strained through an American guarantee to India, we could expect much the same results as from Chinese dissemination of nuclear weapons to China's Asian allies—an extension of nuclear power amongst the USA's allies and a greater degree of alignment amongst smaller Asian countries. Asia would then be, as it is now, the most explosive part of the world; but its explosiveness would be potentially much greater.

It would be impossible to sustain Afro-Asianism under such circumstances; instead, there would presumably be the development of rival brands, one organized by India with American blessing, the other by China. Any unity of approach which Asian states had ever had would disappear, since the issue of colonialism which previously brought them together would have been replaced by a strict alignment between contending powers. There would also, presumably, be a distinct separation from Africa, so far as governments were concerned. African states' first reaction would be to try to dissociate themselves from incipient disaster. China would undoubtedly try to stimulate support from small revolutionary groups, whose purpose would be to attack India and the USA at the international level, and their own governments at the local level. This is, in essence, the line which China takes now. But it would be very much sharpenèd in its identification of India and other associates of the United States with heresy to Afro-Asianism.

It would seem that, so far as the Third World is concerned, the problem of the nuclear balance is essentially that of China. If China disturbs the balance, or causes India to do so, there may be no end to the repercussions. The present Chinese inclination towards subversion of other régimes in Asia and Africa would be extended to the point of endangering not only the régimes but the peaceful development of their countries. For many states this would accelerate the present trend away from militancy and towards a loose accommodation with the Western powers; but for some in Asia it would mean the decision to give in to China, because of the disastrous possibilities of any alternative.

Sino-Soviet relations

The best way to view China's future impact on the Third World is probably in terms of Sino-Soviet relations, because the Soviet Union is China's greatest neighbour, and still presumably the country with which is most preoccupied; and because China and the Soviet Union are continually in competition in the Third World, seeking influence in ways which may encourage either or both to greater intemperance. The Soviet Union is probably the strongest determinant of Chinese actions.

All the present indications suggest that competition will continue between the two for adherence in Africa and Asia. Each will try to influence both states and revolutionary movements, including local Communist parties where those exist. The Soviet Union seems the more likely to succeed with governments, China with militants. This is to be expected, since the Soviet Union has much more to offer governments in the way of economic and military aid, and in that of acceptance of their legitimacy. China, on the other hand, has deliberately set out to court the extreme militants in African and Asian states. The division between the two is not absolute: the Soviet Union is still glad to encourage subversion where this seems likely to do no harm to its national interests, and it has a considerable interest in preserving some loyalty from local Communist parties, especially in the Middle East and India. But, in the stringent circumstances of the struggle between the two powers, which has produced such exhibitions of Chinese arrogance as at Algiers, it is probable that most Afro-Asian countries would give support (though often only tacit support) to the Russian side. Those directly connected with China are, as always, special cases.

The contest for support in the Third World is partly a very serious one, involving questions of the relative strength of China and the Soviet Union, but it also has some of the qualities of a public relations exercise. More fundamental, but less open to speculation because of our lack of effective knowledge, is probably the tension along the extensive Sino-Soviet border. This has relevance for a good many Asian states, especially in the Middle East and Central Asia; it is also of importance to Japan. Open conflict of any sort would be bound to affect these countries. Chinese wooing of Pakistan can be explained in this context as well as in that of the wish to humble India. The Soviet attempt to get approval from neighbouring states, especially in the Middle East, can be interpreted as both a search for Third World sympathy and a search for national security. But our difficulty in analysis is to work out how tense is the situation between the Soviet Union and China, which border areas might be most sensitive, and which issues might provoke action with consequent effects on other Asian states; we simply do not know enough to develop reliable hypotheses, although we can always submit to the temptation to guess. Unless the things which both sides say are entirely divorced from their real intentions, there must be tension; it is reasonable to assume that it is probably greatest over those areas of the Soviet Union which China can claim were filched from it in the nineteenth-century Russian drive for Asian territory. If China ever wants an issue on which it might hope for Afro-Asian sympathy against the Soviet Union, this is it—provided that China has not already acquired such a reputation for deviousness and subversion as to make all its statements suspect.

As with the nuclear balance, the initiative in Sino-Soviet relations seems to lie with China. The basis for a reasonable compromise between the two lies ready to hand, as it does over nuclear weapons. A different Chinese leadership might wish to come to terms with the Soviet Union. Even the present leadership can hardly envisage open war; presumably it finds continual tension a useful source of unity at home and propaganda abroad, but it cannot relish the prospect of superior Russian military technology being exercised against Chinese cities. The Soviet Union is the only major source from which China could hope to get help in the further development of its economy; quite possibly, there will always be voices in Peking urging a rapprochement so that economic concerns could become paramount. Under what conditions the Soviet Union would accept an easing of relations resulting in further Russian investment of knowledge and resources in China is a matter for conjecture. On a long view, there is no inevitable conflict of interests between the two, provided the Chinese adopt the Russian approach of revisionism, especially as regards peaceful coexistence.

The Russian doctrine of coexistence does not, of course, involve giving up encouragement to Communist revolution in other countries. It simply involves the manipulation of that encouragement to suit general Russian policy. If Chinese and Russian interests could be harmonized, the manipulation would suit their joint interests. It could then be quite formidable in certain cases. The damage done in assemblies of Communists and militants by fights between Chinese and Russian spokesmen could be in part repaired; training of cadres could be co-ordinated; much greater flexibility could be introduced into the tactics of individual Communist parties. Similarly, if the two countries came together, they could work out a joint strategy towards national-bourgeois régimes in Africa and Asia. The present degree of competition discredits both of them, although, as already suggested, it probably works in favour of the Soviet Union. Under conditions of harmony, it could be made to work in the interests of both.

If, then, Sino-Soviet relations became easier, to the point of active co-operation instead of enmity, the régimes of the Third World would have much to worry about. So would the United States. It is fashionable to think that, because such a rapprochement could come about only on revisionist (i.e the Soviet Union's) terms, it would mean a general normalization of China's external relations. But this need not be so. China might enter the United Nations and show a rather less ugly face towards the West, but this would be quite compatible, from a Communist standpoint, with further but more subtle attempts to create pro-Communist régimes in Third World countries. Unless relations between the United States and the Soviet Union had become very close indeed, with a degree of mutual trust not experienced so far, such attempts would also suit the Russians. Unless they were to desert altogether the idea of a world Communist movement, they would have to continue to support Communists abroad; and unless they were willing to see more and more Third World states link up with the United States, in military and/or economic terms, they would probably wish to encourage intrigue and subversion which promised more receptive régimes.

We simply do not know which way Sino-Soviet relations will turn. Present indications suggest that they will remain bad, but there is enough possibility of rapprochement to make this a contingency which no interested party can ignore. It is worth emphasizing that this very uncertainty is itself the reason why Sino-Soviet relations constitute one of the most important areas of change in world affairs. As we have seen, a turn towards either better or worse relations could have profound consequences for other states, especially those near the borders of the two powers, but also farther afield. For the peace of mind of most Afro-Asian states, it is probably better that China and the Soviet Union should remain apart, provided this does not cause China to embark on military adventures, or even, perhaps, on nuclear war.

World economics

Every consideration of the future of Third World states must take into account the great differences between their living standards and those of the developed countries, and must hazard some conjecture about whether this gap will prove a significant element of change in their mutual relations. The difficulty is that there is no clear causal connection between economic conditions and political outcomes, in spite of constant efforts to argue to the contrary. As we saw in Chapter 5, it is frequently stated that the poverty of Third World states will lead to their having Communist governments, in spite of the fact that experience so far gives no instance of this having occurred. It is also often stated that the poverty of Third World states provides them with such a vital common interest that they have the strongest incentive to act together to serve it; but, apart from declaratory statements at UNCTAD and in other organs of the UN, the actual tendency amongst Third World states has been towards bilateral bargains with whatever developed countries were prepared to conclude them. It is often implied that the gap can be narrowed or removed by political action by the Western countries; in fact, however, only the direst sacrifice on their part could make any uniform change in living standards throughout the Third World, and nothing can be done that is not difficult, prolonged, and chancy.

Mr Nehru said in January 1963 that, as the colonial experience of the Afro-Asian countries receded, they had to find a new basis for their relations with one another. They had tried to do this through non-alignment. In addition they needed to do this increasingly through cooperation in economic development. That, in his opinion, would be more difficult, and it lay some way in the future.[1]

[1] Jansen, p. 227.

He was quite right. The essence of the Third World difficulty lies in the fact that, unless vast countries like India and Indonesia can become industrialized, as Japan has done, the economic relations of Third World countries will mostly be with those of Europe and North America, where the buying power for their commodities and the means to invest in their economies are concentrated. As things stand, the Western countries are those in which this concentration is greatest. The Soviet Union and Eastern Europe have some of it, but little in comparison with Western Europe and North America. Moreover, Communist planned economies allow little scope for external investment. The idea of deliberately using resources abroad instead of at home is foreign to Communist economics, except for political reasons. The habit of international trade and investment on economic ground is not easily acquired.

Any significant change in this area will, therefore, depend very largely on what the Western powers do. If they fell into the pit of depression, in spite of all their built-in means of avoiding it, they would inflict great damage on the Third World, immediately through inability to pay high prices for its products, and also through inability to invest in it. If they avoided the pit and used their joint efforts to keep up prices, expand technical aid, and strengthen the agencies which promote fruitful investment in Third World countries, they could hope for gradual improvement. But it can only be very gradual indeed.

There is very little that the Third World as a whole can do about this. Individual countries can make better or worse bargains, depending upon their resources, their energy, and their political dispensability. It seems inevitable that the existing process of largely bilateral bargaining should continue, although it is possible that some multilateral agreements may be made along the lines of

UNCTAD's recipes for commodities. At best, this is a possibility. Foreseeable developments in the external economic conditions of Afro-Asian states suggest that these will augment the general tendency towards individual national searches for security and prosperity. A Third World characterized by unity, purpose, and effective tactics is here, as elsewhere, a chimera.